5 the ultimate -ingredient COOKBOOK

Whole Food Flavorful Meals Made Simple

Rebecca White

founder of

A Pleasant Little Kitchen

PAGE STREET
PUBLISHING CO.

PAGE STREET
PUBLISHING CO.

Copyright © 2021 Rebecca White

First published in 2021 by

Page Street Publishing Co.

27 Congress Street, Suite 105

Salem, MA 01970

www.pagestreetpublishing.com

Distributed by Macmillan, sales in Canada by The Canadian Manda Group.

25   24   23   22   21   1   2   3   4   5

ISBN-13: 978-1-64567-310-1

ISBN-10: 1-64567-310-3

Library of Congress Control Number: 2020948569

Cover and book design by Ashley Tenn for Page Street Publishing Co.

Photography by Rebecca White

Printed and bound in China

to Randy, Katherine, Eli, Nancy and Jim

the ones with whom I will always share my table

contents

introduction

Good food is a refuge found in pleasant kitchens, where loved ones gather, visitors are welcomed and daily congregation is ritual. Clutter comes and goes like a healthy dose of shifting sunlight. Busy bodies traverse in and out, dusting the floors with remnants of their presence: a sign that life lives here. This space contains piles of last night's pans and a sink of soiled plates. A lengthy and exceptional meal leads to satisfied diners and a next-day tidy-up.

A scene like this is a charming and most powerful place. It reflects my cooking space where, since 2014, I have dreamed, developed and photographed hundreds of recipes, for not just my online community, but for publications and food media outlets throughout the world.

A self-taught home cook, I actively pursued my then hobby—now career—to reflect the love I have for feeding others. The space from which I cooked, created and congregated was, and still is, a pleasant, little kitchen. Thus, this daily action was married with its location, inspiring my blog name and creating what has become a notable, respected and sought-after food resource. A Pleasant Little Kitchen is where we can all come together to cook side by side to feed the ones we love.

The recipes created from my kitchen encompass wholesome, diverse and seasonal ingredients. My photographs reflect what I see in each plate of food cooked: beautiful nourishment.

Minimal-ingredient cooking is one of the most important skills to have—it allows you to provide quality, homemade meals within the constraints of life. My goal is to help you accomplish this kind of cooking, and *The Ultimate 5-Ingredient Cookbook* is where you and I meet to make a successful dinner plan. Together, we will create a nourishing and sought-after dinner table.

Quality ingredients—coupled with smart techniques—make enjoyable meals. Within this book are recipes and instructions that embody this way of cooking, and it will help you become a successful minimal-ingredient home cook. I hope that my recipes will not only help you to create simple, classic meals, but also to advance your cooking skills. This book provides recipes that will become a platform from which you can spring forward to confidently cook the food you crave, even with only a handful of ingredients.

The following pages are filled with approachable recipes and bold ingredients that yield delicious, balanced food. Recipes will balance the familiar with the unfamiliar. From ground ginger to saffron, mayonnaise to anchovy paste, Dijon to harissa, the variety of ingredients used in these recipes abounds. It is not the quantity of ingredients that anchors this book; it is the thoughtful use and smart application of flavorful ingredients.

When cooking with minimal ingredients, extracting and highlighting flavors from each ingredient is critical. Salt and spices are not the only ways to flavor food. Acid, time and technique also have this capability.

The use of acidic components like vinegars, citrus, tomatoes and wine will be relied upon throughout the book. Many recipes will require time spent either in the oven, fridge or on the cooktop to allow flavors to be extracted and maturate. Utilizing the multiple layers of an ingredient through specific techniques in order to extract flavor will also be employed in these recipes. Why just use fresh orange juice when the zest can also enhance a dish? Do not toss out all the bacon grease from the skillet; use this salty fat to toast breadcrumbs. While melted butter is satisfying, its browned counterpart is divine and decadent—use it occasionally to change a recipe's profile. Each ingredient found in the kitchen is multifaceted—use them as such.

While most of the recipes can be made in just two or three simple steps, some are a bit more in-depth, but well worth the extra time. Whether it is browning meats and tomato paste, simmering shrimp tails in cream or steaming vegetables before roasting, I implore you not to skip these instructions. The result of these additional steps is thoughtful cooking, which yields layers of flavor and exciting meals. Baked Tarragon Lamb Meatballs (page 45) and Dijon Butter Lettuce Salad (page 105) are two of my favorite recipes that require minimal steps to make. Simplistic yet powerful recipes like these fill the pages. Every once in a while, there will be a recipe well worth the extra steps, like the French Onion Beef Stew (page 78). This spin on a classic French onion soup is worth the few added minutes to make.

Take these recipes and make them your own. Cook them exactly as written, or tweak to represent your own preferences and what is available in your pantry.

Three times a day, food is required to fuel you. Found within a well-used kitchen is a beacon that burns vigilantly. It calls out to those who know, or who have heard, that within your space dwells what history has proven to be a most powerful thing: simple, good food.

pantry staples

When the goal is to create flavorful meals with few ingredients, the secret to success is a well-stocked pantry. Having a pantry full of oils, acids, lemons, baking essentials, dried spices and herbs allows you to be efficient and successful in the kitchen. Keeping these basic ingredients handy will prevent trips to the store with a long list of ingredients for each meal.

My five-ingredient recipes are built off the following pantry staples. To easily execute each recipe, a handful of stocked basics will be needed along with five additional ingredients. Do not worry if the current state of your pantry is bare. With each new recipe cooked, more ingredients will be added, expanding your pantry as well as your ingredient knowledge. Here are all the items I consider pantry essentials and assume you will have readily available when making these recipes.

- black pepper
- canola oil
- dried oregano
- dried red pepper flakes
- dried thyme
- extra-virgin olive oil
- flour
- granulated garlic
- ground cinnamon
- ground ginger
- honey
- kosher salt
- lemon
- red wine vinegar
- sugar
- unsalted butter
- white wine vinegar

savory chicken

Quick to cook and neutral in flavor, chicken is a go-to protein that can be found on many weekly menus. From braising to broiling, there are many ways a chicken can be cooked to create satisfying and flavorful meals.

The most reliable and accurate way to ensure perfectly cooked chicken is to use an instant read thermometer to monitor the internal temperature. While chicken is considered fully cooked at 165°F (74°C), there are times that the chicken should be removed from the heat early to prevent overcooking, like in the Chicken Olive-Marsala (page 20). On the other hand, Rosemary-Orange Spatchcock Chicken (page 12) should remain in the oven until it reaches doneness. Make sure to always read the Cooking Notes to prevent the dreaded dry bird. I provide tips to help you cook your chicken perfectly every time.

Half of the chicken recipes found in this chapter are one-pan meals—a glorious approach to cooking. To create successful one-pan meals, it is important to use powerful ingredients, allow flavors to develop and include a variety of textures. Baked Cardamom Chicken Skewers with Saffron Rice (page 15) requires minimal prep and uses cardamom and saffron as the flavor base. The broil at the end allows the top layer of rice to become crispy while the rice underneath remains perfectly fluffy. The cooking preparation for the Roasted Chicken and Smothered Peppered Cabbage (page 16) creates a salty, crispy chicken skin with peppered and creamy cabbage.

The remaining half of the chicken recipes are entrées that will need side dishes. The Rosemary-Orange Spatchcock Chicken (page 12) pairs beautifully with the Dijon Butter Lettuce Salad (page 105), and the Tomato and Horseradish–Braised Chicken Thighs (page 24) with its unique sauce begs for Rosemary Garlic Sour Cream Mashed Potatoes (page 114). Old Bay Baked Chicken Wings (page 27) can become a one-pan meal by simply adding a vegetable— I recommend small round potatoes or broccolini—to the sheet pan when roasting the wings.

Chicken does not have to be boneless, skinless and tasteless. Thoughtfully cooked chicken can be a mealtime highlight, anchoring a dinner plate and becoming a reliable go-to staple.

Rosemary-Orange Spatchcock Chicken

Easier to prepare than a whole roasted chicken, spatchcocked chicken is also worthy of the "wow" factor that whole roasting gets. With a quick sear in a skillet and then a 30-minute oven roast, cooking with a spatchcock chicken is a straight-forward technique. This Rosemary-Orange Spatchcock Chicken is coated with an orange zest butter, yielding a rich and decadent roasted bird full of citrus and herb notes. This chicken is sure to be requested often.

Cooking Notes:

- *Remember to zest the oranges before juicing. If ½ cup (120 ml) of juice cannot be extracted from the oranges, that's okay. Extract as much as you can.*

- *To salt the chicken under the skin, the skin will need to be partially detached from the meat. Grab an edge of the skin and lift slightly. This should expose a small area where the skin is still attached to the meat. Using a knife, gently make a couple of small slices through this area. Using your finger, gently separate the meat and skin. Peel the skin back, being careful to not completely remove the skin from the chicken meat. Salt the exposed meat and return the peeled-back skin to its original position.*

Yields 4–6 SERVINGS

2 oranges, zest and juice

2 tbsp (28 g) unsalted butter, softened

1¼ tsp (8 g) kosher salt, divided

3½ lb (1.6 kg) spatchcock chicken

7 rosemary sprigs, divided

1 tbsp (15 ml) extra-virgin olive oil

1 large yellow onion, peeled and cut into large chunks

½ cup (120 ml) low-sodium chicken stock

Heat the oven to 450°F (232°C).

After zesting both oranges, juice one orange, yielding about ½ cup (120 ml) of juice, then slice the other orange into wedges. Set the juice and the orange wedges aside. Combine the orange zest and the butter. Stir and set aside.

Using 2 tablespoons (28 g) of the orange zest butter and 1 teaspoon of the salt, evenly coat the outside and under the skin of the chicken. While the chicken skin is peeled back, place 4 rosemary sprigs (1 for each breast, and 1 for each leg and thigh) on top of the chicken meat. Pull the skin over the rosemary and set aside.

Place the oil and onion into a large cast-iron skillet. Warm over medium-high heat and cook the onion for 3 minutes, or until it is slightly softened and coated with a layer of pan juices. Push the onion to the perimeter of the skillet and add the chicken, breast side facing down. Cook for 2½ minutes, then flip the chicken. Add the orange slices and the remaining 3 sprigs of rosemary to the skillet. Cook for 2½ minutes.

Place the skillet into the oven. Roast for 30 minutes or until the chicken reaches an internal temperature of 160°F to 165°F (71°C to 74°C). Remove the skillet from the oven, place the chicken onto a cutting board, cover with foil and let rest for 10 minutes.

Return the skillet back to the cooktop and warm over medium-high heat. Add the chicken stock, orange juice and ¼ teaspoon of the salt to the skillet and bring to a boil. Boil for 2 to 3 minutes, stirring occasionally. Remove from the heat. Slice the chicken and serve with the pan sauce.

Baked Cardamom Chicken Skewers with Saffron Rice

This Middle Eastern–inspired dish uses sweetly aromatic cardamom and cinnamon as the base flavors for the yogurt marinade. A 24-hour marinade in this tangy, fragrant yogurt allows the chicken skewers to become very tender, and marinating the day before cooking allows for dinner to be made quickly. Baked on top of earthy saffron rice, this dish is a spin on the American classic, Chicken and Rice.

Cooking Notes:

- *Cut the chicken into evenly sized pieces to ensure even cooking.*

- *Be sure to thoroughly pat the chicken dry to remove all the yogurt marinade. There is plenty of marinade if you want to increase the amount of chicken used.*

Yields 4–6 SERVINGS

1 cup (258 g) plain yogurt

½ tsp ground cinnamon

1½ tsp (5 g) ground cardamom

2 tsp (12 g) kosher salt, divided

5 tbsp (75 ml) olive oil, divided

1½ lb (680 g) chicken, cut into 2-inch (5-cm) cubes

2 cups (414 g) basmati rice

3½ cups (840 ml) water

¼ tsp saffron, crumbled

Lemon wedges, for serving

For the table: Pickled Red Onions (page 124)

In a large bowl, combine the yogurt, cinnamon, cardamom, 1 teaspoon of the salt and 2 tablespoons (30 ml) of the oil. Stir to combine. Add the chicken pieces and stir to coat. Cover and store in the fridge for at least 6 hours and up to 24 hours.

When ready to cook, heat the oven to 425°F (218°C). Put the rice in a large rectangular ceramic baking dish. Place the water, 3 tablespoons (45 ml) of the oil and 1 teaspoon of the salt into a pan and bring to a boil. Once boiling, pour the water over the rice. Add the saffron to the mixture and stir. Place into the oven and cook for 30 minutes, or until the rice is soft and fluffy.

While the rice is cooking, remove the chicken from the fridge and pat dry with paper towels. Place the chicken onto skewers and set aside.

After the rice has cooked for 30 minutes, remove it from the oven and place the skewers on top of the rice. Return to the oven and cook for 15 minutes, or until the chicken reaches an internal temperature of 165°F (74°C). Turn on the broiler and brown for 1 minute. Remove from the oven and serve warm with a squeeze of fresh lemon juice.

Roasted Chicken and Smothered Peppered Cabbage

The simplicity of this dish is fantastic. It is a one-pan, hassle-free meal. If you can find preshredded cabbage, it will make this dish even easier to make. The fat from the chicken skin seasons the cabbage and creates a decadent skillet meal. I add the cabbage and onion mixture directly in the skillet—which minimizes equipment and cleanup—but you can also use a large bowl if you prefer. This is the type of meal that you can prep and then clean while it is cooking. While the cabbage is cooking for the first 15 minutes, salt the chicken and tidy the cooking area. Once the chicken goes into the oven, continue to tidy up or prep another side dish.

Cooking Notes:

- *This recipe works best when the chicken is all the same cut. If you prefer chicken breasts, use them. Chicken breasts will take less time to cook, so adjust the time accordingly.*

- *If cooking for a group who likes white and dark meat, do not fret. Combine the cuts and remove the breasts a few minutes before the thighs. Use an oven-safe thermometer to monitor the temperature for doneness.*

Yields 4–6 SERVINGS

1 head cabbage (about 2 lb [907 g]), thinly sliced

1 small yellow onion, diced

5 cloves garlic, thinly sliced

2 tbsp (30 ml) extra-virgin olive oil, divided

1 tsp fresh black pepper

2 tsp (12 g) kosher salt, divided

1 tbsp (15 ml) red wine vinegar

3 lb (1.4 kg) bone-in and skin-on chicken thighs

For the table: Pickled Red Onions (page 124) and Garlic Coeur à la Crème (page 128)

Heat the oven to 425°F (218°C).

Place the cabbage, onion and garlic into a cast-iron skillet. Top with 1 tablespoon (15 ml) of the oil, the pepper, 1 teaspoon of the salt and the vinegar. Toss to combine. Place into the oven and roast for 15 minutes.

While the cabbage cooks, place the chicken onto a cutting board and drizzle 1 tablespoon (15 ml) of the oil over all sides. It is fine if you don't need to use all of the oil. Sprinkle 1 teaspoon of the salt evenly on and under the chicken skin. For tips on salting chicken under the skin, see the cooking notes for Rosemary-Orange Spatchcock Chicken (page 12).

Remove the skillet from the oven and place the chicken on top of the cabbage. Place the skillet back into the oven and cook for 33 to 42 minutes, or until the chicken reaches an internal temperature of 165°F (74°C). Remove from the oven and let cool for 10 minutes. Serve the chicken sliced or whole with the cabbage.

Chicken and Couscous with 20 Cloves of Garlic

A play off the classic—albeit labor intensive—French Chicken with 40 Cloves of Garlic, this 20-clove version provides the same traditional flavor of the beloved dish but in a more approachable way. Cooking couscous directly with the chicken makes it a wonderful one-pan meal.

Cooking Notes:

- *Do not use boneless, skinless chicken breasts for this as the recipe timing will not work. Avoid large or unevenly sized chicken breasts. Smaller, similarly sized chicken breasts will cook more evenly. If using small chicken breasts, err on the lower end of the cook times.*

- *Make sure to pull back the chicken skin to salt the meat. Salting only the skin makes briny skin—not seasoned chicken. If more chicken is desired, increase the number of breasts to four, add a smidge more salt and sear the breasts in two batches. The cook time of the couscous will ultimately be determined by how long it takes for the chicken breasts to braise.*

Yields 4 SERVINGS

1¼ tsp (8 g) kosher salt, divided

3 bone-in, skin-on chicken breasts (about 2¼ lb [1 kg])

1 tbsp (15 ml) extra-virgin olive oil

¼ cup (60 ml) cognac

4 cups (960 ml) low-sodium chicken stock, plus more as needed

20 cloves garlic, peels removed

¼ tsp dried thyme (or 3 to 4 sprigs fresh thyme)

2 tbsp (28 g) unsalted butter

1⅓ cups (224 g) pearl couscous

Evenly distribute 1 teaspoon of the salt onto the chicken and under the skin. For tips on salting chicken under the skin, see the Rosemary-Orange Spatchcock Chicken (page 12) cooking notes. In a flat-bottom skillet wide enough to hold three chicken breasts and deep enough to hold and boil 4 cups (960 ml) of liquid, heat the oil over medium-high heat for about 3 minutes. Brown the chicken, 3 to 4 minutes per side. Remove from the skillet and set aside. Add the cognac, stock, garlic, ¼ teaspoon of the salt, thyme and butter to the skillet and stir. Once the butter has melted, return the chicken to the pan. The chicken should be about three-quarters of the way covered. If it is not, add more stock. Bring to a boil and then reduce the heat to low. Cover and simmer for 15 minutes, or until the chicken reaches an internal temperature of 140°F (60°C).

Add the couscous to the skillet and stir. Be sure that the couscous is dispersed into the cooking liquid and not resting on top of the chicken. Simmer, covered, for 3 to 5 minutes. Remove the lid and check the temperature of the chicken. If cooked to 160°F (71°C), set aside and cover with foil. Continue cooking the couscous uncovered for 5 to 10 minutes or until the liquid is mostly absorbed. If the chicken is not cooked through, cover and continue to simmer until it reaches 160°F (71°C). Remove the chicken and rest for 5 minutes. Slice the chicken and serve with the couscous.

Chicken Olive-Marsala

Olives and Marsala are well matched for each other. Served alongside a nicely crusted chicken, this is a really good plate of food. Chicken Olive-Marsala is briny and tangy—a balanced and satisfying meal with only a few ingredients. If you want to save a bit of time and can find thinly sliced boneless, skinless chicken breasts at the store, use them.

Cooking Notes:

- *I like to remove the chicken from the pan when it reaches an internal temperature of about 160°F (71°C). It helps ensure that the chicken does not overcook and get tough.*

- *While the cook time for the chicken is under 15 minutes, Chicken Olive-Marsala is not a "throw in the pan and walk away" recipe. It takes supervision because of the short cook time needed for the halved chicken breasts. I suggest pairing this recipe with a glass of wine and some topics to contemplate while cooking.*

- *The first batch of chicken will cook a bit slower than the second batch, simply because the pan will not be as hot. If the butter begins to burn, reduce the heat. When selecting the Marsala, be sure to choose one labeled as dry, not sweet. If there are fresh herbs in your fridge, like basil or parsley, use them to top the chicken before serving.*

Yields 6 SERVINGS

¾ tsp salt

3 boneless, skinless chicken breasts (about 2 lb [907 g]), halved into cutlets

2 to 3 tbsp (28 to 42 g) unsalted butter, divided

½ cup (79 g) flour

½ cup (80 g) diced shallots

1 cup (240 ml) dry Marsala

¼ cup (60 ml) balsamic vinegar

½ cup (73 g) chopped olives (or more to taste)

Evenly distribute the salt on the chicken breasts. Set aside.

In a large flat-bottomed skillet, heat 1 tablespoon (14 g) of the butter over medium heat, about 3 minutes.

Working in batches of 2 to 3 cutlets at a time, dredge the chicken in the flour. Gently shake the chicken to remove excess flour. Add the chicken to the pan, making sure to not crowd the pan, and cook 3 minutes per side, or until the chicken reaches an internal temperature of 160°F (71°C). Remove the cooked chicken and repeat the steps with the second batch, making sure to use an additional 1 tablespoon (14 g) of the butter. Continue with the remaining chicken, if necessary.

Reduce the heat to low. Add the shallots and cook for 30 seconds, stirring constantly. Deglaze the skillet with the Marsala, making sure to scrape up any browned pieces stuck to the bottom of the pan. Add the vinegar and stir to combine. Let the sauce simmer for 5 minutes, or until slightly reduced. Stir in the olives and add the chicken back to the pan to coat with the sauce. Serve the chicken with pan sauce.

To add extra flavor, *top with fresh lemon juice.*

Sheet-Pan Cumin Chicken and Bell Peppers

Good sheet-pan meals are weeknight necessities. The broiler speeds the cooking process along tremendously, which makes this particular recipe a gem. Sheet-Pan Cumin Chicken and Bell Peppers is hearty enough to be eaten by itself, but is also good in tortillas or buns, over rice or with a side of chips.

Cooking Notes:

- *The mayonnaise is a quick marinade and adds not only salt but also umami to the chicken.*
- *The cook time will vary depending upon how thick the chicken slices are cut. To make fewer servings, use ¾ to 1 pound (340 to 454 g) of chicken and use only 2 bell peppers. If the broiler does not go up to 550°F (288°C), adjust the temperature to its highest setting.*

Yields 4–6 SERVINGS

¼ cup (52 g) mayonnaise

1 tbsp plus 2 tsp (12 g) cumin

1 tsp kosher salt, plus more as needed, divided

1½ lb (680 g) chicken tenders, thinly sliced

1 large yellow onion, halved and thinly sliced

3 bell peppers (about ¾ lb [340 g]), cored, seeded and thinly sliced

2 tsp (10 ml) canola oil

2 tsp (10 ml) white wine vinegar

For the table: Pickled Red Onions (page 124)

In a large mixing bowl, combine the mayonnaise, cumin and ¾ teaspoon of the salt. Mix well. Add the chicken and stir to coat. Cover and marinate at room temperature for 30 minutes.

Place the oven rack to the highest slot in the oven. Heat the broiler to 550°F (288°C).

While the chicken is marinating, line a sheet pan with foil and add the onion and bell peppers. Top evenly with the oil and ¼ teaspoon of the salt. Toss to incorporate. Spread the mixture out into one even layer. Broil for 4 to 5 minutes. Stir the vegetables and continue to broil for 4 to 5 minutes or until the vegetables are slightly browned and blistered.

Remove the sheet pan from the oven and toss the vegetables. Add the vinegar to the chicken and toss to coat. With tongs, add the chicken tenders to the sheet pan in an even layer on top of the vegetables.

Broil for 5 to 7 minutes, or until the chicken reaches an internal temperature of 165°F (74°C).

Remove the sheet pan from the oven. Salt to taste. Serve with your favorite sides.

To add extra flavor, *top with lime wedges and cilantro.*

Tomato and Horseradish–Braised Chicken Thighs

This is a unique dish that utilizes a few ingredients and cooking techniques to create a comforting meal. The horseradish and tomatoes, when cooked together, create a sauce perfect for braising chicken thighs. The lemon juice and zest complement the braising sauce and help to tie the dish together.

Cooking Notes:

- *Chicken thighs tend to have quite a bit of excess skin. When braising, this skin can become unpleasant, so I like to remove a good portion with kitchen shears. I leave just enough to cover the thigh meat. Don't forget to salt the meat under the skin. Remember, the larger the thigh, the longer the cook time will be.*

- *Be sure to zest the lemons before extracting the juice. If there are any fresh herbs in your fridge, like basil or tarragon, use them as a topping when serving the chicken.*

Yields 4–6 SERVINGS

2 tsp (12 g) kosher salt, divided

6 to 8 chicken thighs (about 3½ lb [1.6 kg]), excess skin trimmed

2 tbsp (30 ml) extra-virgin olive oil

1 cup (240 ml) low-sodium chicken stock

1 (28-oz [794-g]) can whole tomatoes

3 tbsp (45 g) horseradish

2 lemons (zest from 2 lemons and juice from 1 lemon)

1 tbsp (10 g) flour

For the table: Herbed Crème Fraiche (page 123)

Heat the oven to 375°F (191°C).

Evenly distribute 1½ teaspoons (9 g) of the salt on the chicken thighs. Be sure to salt under the skin. For tips on salting chicken under the skin, see the cooking notes for the Rosemary-Orange Spatchcock Chicken (page 12).

Add the oil to a Dutch oven or braising pan and warm over medium-high heat. Once the oil is hot, about 4 minutes, add the chicken thighs to the pan, skin side down. Cook for 2 to 3 minutes, or until the skin is golden. Flip and brown the other side for 2 to 3 minutes. Remove the chicken from the pan and set aside. Depending on the size of the pan, this may have to be done in two batches.

Lower the heat to medium and add the chicken stock. Deglaze the pan, being sure to scrape up any pieces stuck to the bottom of the pan. Add the tomatoes, horseradish, ½ teaspoon of the salt, the lemon zest and juice. Stir well to combine. Return the chicken and its juices to the pan. Place the pan into the oven and cook for 20 to 25 minutes, or until the chicken reaches an internal temperature of 165°F (74°C).

Remove the chicken and cover with foil to keep warm. Scoop out the tomatoes, place into a blender and puree. Add the flour to the blended tomatoes and blitz until well combined. Pour the tomato mixture back into the braising pan and place onto the cooktop. Simmer on medium-low heat for 15 minutes to thicken. Serve the chicken topped with the sauce.

Old Bay Baked Chicken Wings

I have tried several cooking methods for baked wings. This approach is the least messy and time consuming, and it yields a crispy wing with an outstanding flavor from the Old Bay Seasoning. If I'm not careful, I could consume an entire sheet pan of these wings—they are that good. And if I'm honest, I often double this recipe because it is simple to make and incredibly delicious.

Cooking Notes:

- *This is a foolproof method for crispy baked wings—just remember to allow the wings to rest in the fridge for 4 to 24 hours before cooking. If you make them the night before and set them in the fridge to rest, they'll make a super easy hands-off dinner the next night.*

- *Depending on your love of wings, 2 pounds (907 g) of drumettes may not be enough. This is not a problem—simply double the recipe, but do not double the salt. I have found that slightly overcooking drumettes—and other dark chicken meat—to about 175°F (79°C) makes for a firmer texture, which I prefer.*

Yields 2–4 SERVINGS

3½ tsp (16 g) Old Bay Seasoning, divided

⅛ tsp kosher salt

1½ tsp (6 g) baking powder

2 lb (907 g) chicken drumettes

For the table: Pickled Red Onions (page 124) and Garlic Coeur à la Crème (page 128)

In a large bowl, thoroughly combine 2½ teaspoons (12 g) of the Old Bay Seasoning, the salt and baking powder. Set aside.

Using paper towels, pat the chicken dry and place into the bowl with the seasoning. Toss the wings to thoroughly coat with the seasoning.

Place a cooling rack on a foil-lined rimmed sheet pan. Add the chicken to the rack and place into the refrigerator. Chill for at least 4 hours, and up to 24 hours.

Heat the oven to 450°F (232°C). Cook the wings for 35 to 40 minutes or until the chicken reaches 165°F (74°C), flipping halfway through baking to ensure evenly crispy skin.

Remove the chicken from the oven and toss in the pan with the remaining 1 teaspoon of the Old Bay Seasoning. Serve immediately.

hearty beef, pork and lamb

Beef, pork and lamb vary greatly in flavor and how best to cook. In this chapter, there is one-pan cooking, as well as multipan extravaganzas. Choose whichever recipe is right for the moment—and save the others for another day.

If craving a weeknight steak, the Skillet Beef Tenderloin with Garlic Broccolini (page 33) is a one-pan dinner that yields a perfectly pink tenderloin in 45 minutes, thanks to the reverse sear method of cooking. If low, slow comfort is desired, the Braised Star Anise Short Ribs (page 30) will satisfy your craving and leave you wanting more. This dish is full of umami and the essence of star anise makes the short ribs memorable, both for their fall-apart tenderness and their refined flavor.

Bacon Brown-Sugared Pork Tenderloin (page 38) is a make-ahead recipe that marinates pork with brown sugar and Dijon before a quick 30-minute cook. This recipe is perfect for a weeknight meal, and can become a sheet-pan dinner by adding vegetables to the pan before roasting. Pork shoulder is practically flawless when slow cooked. One of my all-time favorite recipes is Green Chile–Braised Pork Shoulder (page 37). A slow braise in green chiles and beer yields tender, flavorful (and freezer-friendly) pork that pairs well with tortillas or served over rice.

Fancy in appearance and name—but a cinch to prep and cook—is the Pan-Seared Lamb Chops with Shallots and Mushrooms (page 42). This skillet meal infuses the cooking oil with shallots and rosemary, permeating the entire dish. A slow-cooked lamb dish that I often crave during the week is the Braised Lamb Shoulder with Orzo (page 46). Minimal effort is needed to craft a comforting umami-filled bowl of lamb and pasta.

From braising to baking, from star anise to anchovy paste, this chapter contains a variety of cooking methods and ingredients to create unique, flavorful meals. Recipes found in this chapter will meet your dinner needs on any given day.

Braised Star Anise Short Ribs

Making delicious, tender short ribs is deceivingly easy and requires little from the cook. For this low and slow comfort meal, a quick sear and browning is the only requirement to lay the foundation for a standout—albeit simple—entrée. The braise in the oven creates a deeply flavored meal. The star anise is the "star" of this recipe; this warm and fragrant seed blends beautifully in the sauce, creating an extremely satisfying meal.

Cooking Notes:

- *Star anise can be a very strong flavor. Similar to a cinnamon stick, star anise should be used sparingly and given time to permeate the ingredients with which it cooks. If you haven't used star anise before, start with 2 pods, then add another the next time you braise short ribs if more anise flavor is desired.*

- *Collect rendered fat from the pan twice: once after the short ribs are browned, and again after the short ribs are braised. Gently insert a shallow spoon just under the surface of the simmering gravy and discard the fat into a bowl.*

Yields 4–6 SERVINGS

2 tsp (12 g) kosher salt, divided

3½ lb (1.6 kg) short ribs (8 to 9 ribs)

½ tsp extra-virgin olive oil

1 large yellow onion, finely diced

2 tbsp (32 g) tomato paste

3 cups (720 ml) beef stock

½ tsp dried thyme

1 tsp red wine vinegar

2 to 3 star anise pods

1 tbsp plus 1 tsp (15 g) flour

For the table: Browned Butter Toast (page 120) and Pickled Red Onions (page 124)

Heat the oven to 350°F (177°C). Use 1½ teaspoons (9 g) of the salt to evenly season the short ribs on all sides.

In a large Dutch oven, warm the oil over medium-high heat. Once hot, about 4 minutes, add half of the short ribs to the pan, meaty side down, and brown for 3 minutes. Brown the remaining sides of the short ribs, turning every so often, for an additional 3 minutes. Be sure to get an even sear. Set aside. Add the remaining short ribs to the pan and repeat the browning steps. If the pan gets too hot, turn down the heat accordingly. The entire browning process should take 6 minutes per batch.

Decrease the heat to medium-low and remove the pan from the heat. Pour out all but 1 teaspoon of the fat. Add the onion to the pan and cook off the heat for 2 minutes, stirring frequently. Return the pan to the heat, add the tomato paste and brown for 2 minutes. Add the stock and deglaze the pan, scraping up any browned bits. Add the thyme, vinegar, star anise and ½ teaspoon of the salt. Mix well.

Return the short ribs to the pan. The ribs should be just over halfway submerged in the liquid. If they are not, add water. Bring to a boil, cover and place into the oven. Cook for 2½ to 3 hours, or until the short ribs are tender.

Turn the cooktop to medium-low. Remove the pan from the oven and place onto the cooktop. Spoon off 2 to 3 tablespoons (30 to 45 ml) of the rendered fat, or more if desired. Remove the short ribs, place onto a serving platter and cover.

Remove 1 cup (240 ml) of the cooking liquid and place into a small bowl. Add the flour to the liquid and whisk until the flour has dissolved, creating a slurry. Pour the slurry back into the pan and stir to combine. Simmer the cooking liquid until the sauce has thickened to a gravy-like consistency. Serve the short ribs warm topped with the gravy.

Skillet Beef Tenderloin with Garlic Broccolini

While beef tenderloin can be a splurge, it is my preferred cut of beef. Free from the gristle and toughness often found in other cuts, tenderloin will melt in your mouth when properly cooked. This recipe may sound fancy, but it is an attainable weeknight meal due to the minimal prep required, simple cooking process and easy cleanup.

Cooking Notes:

- *This recipe uses the reverse sear method to cook the steaks since it takes the guesswork out of doneness and guarantees a perfectly cooked steak every time. Don't be alarmed if it takes time for the steaks to heat up. Use the following guidelines to determine doneness:*

  130 to 135°F (54 to 57°C) for medium-rare
  135 to 140°F (57 to 60°C) for medium
  145 to 150°F (63 to 66°C) for medium-well
  155°F (68°C) for well-done

- *Broccolini and broccoli rabe are not the same ingredient. Broccoli rabe has a bitter taste and will not work as an alternative. For a broccolini substitute, use broccoli. However, the broccoli might take a few more minutes to cook.*

Yields 4–6 SERVINGS

4 (6-oz [170-g]) beef tenderloin steaks

4 tsp (20 ml) extra-virgin olive oil, divided

1 tsp kosher salt, plus more to taste

¼ tsp ground black pepper

8 cups (680 g) broccolini, cut into bite-sized pieces

5 cloves garlic, thinly sliced

1 lemon (zest from the entire lemon and juice from half of the lemon)

2 tbsp (30 ml) water

For the table: Browned Butter Toast (page 120)

Heat the oven to 250°F (121°C).

Place the steaks in a cast-iron skillet or a heavy-bottomed oven-safe skillet. Evenly distribute 2 teaspoons (10 ml) of the oil onto both sides of the steaks. Sprinkle the salt and pepper over all sides.

Insert an oven-safe thermometer into the center of the thickest steak. Cook until the thermometer reads 2 to 3 degrees less than the desired doneness, about 45 minutes for medium-rare.

Remove the skillet from the oven and place onto the cooktop. Remove the steaks and place onto a plate. Cover with foil.

Turn the cooktop to medium-high. Add the remaining 2 teaspoons (10 ml) of oil into the pan. Once the oil is shimmering, 3 to 4 minutes, place the steaks into the skillet and sear for 45 seconds to 1 minute. Flip the steaks and sear the other sides for another 45 seconds to 1 minute. The goal is to create a browned crust. Remove the steaks to a serving platter and cover.

Reduce the heat to medium. Place the broccolini into the skillet and stir to coat in the oil. Sauté for 4 minutes or until the broccolini has browned and cooked to al dente. Stir occasionally to prevent burning.

Add the garlic, lemon zest and juice to the pan, stirring constantly for 45 seconds. Deglaze the pan with the water. Continue to stir until the water has reduced and the pan is almost dry, 1 to 2 minutes.

Place the broccolini and garlic on the serving dish with the steaks, and salt to taste. Serve warm.

Tamarind and Lime–Browned Pork

Tangy, tart and unique in flavor, this tamarind pork is an uncomplicated dish that can be served in a variety of ways—on lettuce or rice, or in nachos or tacos. Tamarind paste is one of my favorite ingredients to incorporate tart and savory notes into a dish. This condiment provides instant flavor to vegetables and proteins and is perfect for quick marinades and sauces. Fresh lime juice is always a great complement to use with tamarind.

Cooking Notes:

- *Tamarind paste comes in various preparations. My favorite is an already strained version that only needs to be dissolved quickly in warm water before use. Be sure to read the product instructions before following the steps in this recipe. Not all tamarind paste is the same.*

- *The more browned you get the pork during the cooking process, the more umami that will develop.*

Yields 4–6 SERVINGS

1½ tbsp (38 g) tamarind paste

⅓ cup (80 ml) water, warm to hot

2 tbsp (30 ml) canola oil

10 oz (283 g) chopped mushrooms

1¼ tsp (8 g) kosher salt, divided, plus more to taste

5 cloves garlic, chopped

1½ lb (680 g) ground pork

1½ tsp (4 g) ground ginger

½ tsp white wine vinegar

1 tsp fresh lime juice

In a small bowl, dissolve the tamarind paste in the warm water. Stir and set aside.

Place the oil into a flat-bottomed skillet and warm over medium heat. Once warm, about 3 minutes, add the mushrooms and ½ teaspoon of the salt. Cook for 8 minutes, stirring occasionally. Add the garlic to the skillet and cook until fragrant, about 30 seconds.

Increase the heat to medium-high. Add the pork, ¾ teaspoon of the salt and the ginger. Stir to combine and cook until the pork is browned, 10 to 12 minutes. Stir occasionally. Deglaze the pan with the tamarind liquid, being sure to scrape up any browned bits. Stir in the vinegar.

Remove from the heat and cool for 5 minutes. Add lime juice and salt to taste. Serve wrapped in lettuce leaves or with jasmine rice.

To add more flavor, *add a splash of sesame oil when cooking and top with fresh cilantro or basil.*

Green Chile–Braised Pork Shoulder

This dish is a hassle-free family favorite and can always be found in my freezer. The steps in this recipe are simple, which gives reason to rejoice. Green chiles, garlic, beer, water and pork are simmered low and slow for a couple hours for a truly delicious outcome. This recipe encourages you to serve the pork with tortillas or rice, but keep in mind that it also goes well served on bread for sandwiches, in scrambled eggs for migas or on tortilla chips for nachos. Be creative and serve it according to your cravings—or what is available in your pantry.

Cooking Notes:

- *If you can find freshly roasted Hatch green chiles in July, August or September, I highly suggest using them. If you do not have access to fresh chiles, canned chopped green chiles will also work.*

- *This recipe calls for boneless pork shoulder. Bone-in pork shoulder is also okay to use; however, be sure to select a heavier piece to account for the bone. If a bone-in pork shoulder is used, save the bone and freeze to use for flavoring other dishes. If you have an aversion to handling raw meat, enlist the help of your butcher or someone else at home to cut the pork.*

- *Avoid cooking this dish in a slow cooker. The last step of simmering allows the pork to develop umami by reducing the sauce and browning the meat. Using a slow cooker will eliminate this step and lead to a wet mess of pork.*

Yields 8 SERVINGS

1½ to 2 cups (405 to 540 g) roasted Hatch green chiles, chopped

5 cloves garlic, crushed

12 oz (355 ml) Mexican lager beer, at room temperature

1 cup (240 ml) water

1½ tsp (9 g) kosher salt

3½ to 4 lb (1.6 to 1.8 kg) boneless pork shoulder, cut into 2-inch (5-cm) cubes

Tortillas or cooked rice (for serving)

For the table: Pickled Red Onions (page 124)

Place the chiles, garlic, beer, water and salt into a large Dutch oven and stir to combine. Place the pork into the mixture and bring to a boil over medium-high heat.

Once boiling, reduce the heat to low and bring to a simmer. Cover and cook for 60 to 80 minutes or until the pork is easily pierced with a fork. Stir occasionally.

Remove the lid and continue to cook for 45 to 60 minutes, stirring occasionally to prevent burning. Once most of the liquid is absorbed and the pork is tender and browned, the pork is done.

Serve with tortillas or rice. If desired, add a dollop of sour cream, chopped cilantro and a squeeze of lime juice.

Bacon Brown-Sugared Pork Tenderloin

Sweet and savory, this pork tenderloin can grace a casual weeknight table or be the star of a celebratory meal. The 4-hour marinade makes this desirable for a busy weeknight or a dinner party because when you're ready to cook, more than half the work has already occurred. Come cook time, all that is left to do is a quick 20-minute roast in the oven. Serve this decadent dish with a simple, refreshing side like the Arugula and Grape Cilantro Salad (page 117) and you will have an uncomplicated and outstanding meal.

Cooking Notes:

- *If pork tenderloins larger than 1¼ pounds (567 g) are used, increase the cook time until the tenderloin is cooked all the way through. The amount of bacon used to top the pork will vary based on the size of the pork. If your broiler does not reach 550°F (287°C), use its highest setting.*

Yields 5–6 SERVINGS

1 tsp granulated garlic

1½ tsp (9 g) kosher salt

2 (1¼-lb [567-g]) pork tenderloins

¼ cup (60 ml) Dijon mustard

4 cloves garlic, chopped

½ cup (105 g) plus 1 tbsp (13 g) brown sugar, divided, plus additional to finish

5 to 10 bacon slices (½ lb [227 g]), cut in half

For the table: Pickled Red Onions (page 124) and Garlic Coeur à la Crème (page 128)

In a small bowl, combine the granulated garlic and salt. Stir well to combine.

With a paper towel, pat the two pork tenderloins dry. Place the pork tenderloins on a foil-lined baking sheet. Evenly coat the tenderloins with the salt mixture and then with the mustard. Evenly distribute the garlic and ½ cup (105 g) of the brown sugar on the tenderloins. Make sure all sides are coated with the mustard and brown sugar.

Lay five bacon halves (or as many are needed to cover) on top of the pork tenderloins. Cover with foil and place into the fridge for at least 4 hours.

About 30 minutes prior to cooking, remove the pork from the fridge and heat the oven to 425°F (218°C). Place the pork on a cooling rack on top of a rimmed baking sheet.

Cook for 20 to 25 minutes, or until the pork has reached an internal temperature of 135°F (57°C). Turn off the oven, sprinkle 1 tablespoon (13 g) of the brown sugar on the pork and turn on the broiler to 550°F (288°C). Broil for 2 to 3 minutes or until the bacon is crispy and the pork is at 140°F (60°C). Remove and let sit for 10 minutes.

Slice and serve warm with additional brown sugar, to taste.

To add more flavor, *add red pepper flakes and fresh thyme to the tenderloin seasoning.*

Tomato and Prosciutto Tart

Puff pastry is an ingredient I try to always have in the freezer. This dough can easily create delicious meals or sides with some of the most basic of ingredients. Fresh veggies, a touch of cheese and a few bits of seasoning go a long way with puff pastry. A warm slice or two of this Tomato and Prosciutto Tart—paired with the Dijon Butter Lettuce Salad (page 105) and a glass of red wine—makes for a most pleasant meal.

Cooking Notes:

- *There are several varieties of puff pastry. The type I use has two 9-inch (23-cm) sheets. To make this tart, I simply combine the two sheets together. The size will vary depending on the puff pastry purchased.*

Yields 4 SERVINGS

2 sheets of puff pastry (1.1 lb [499 g]) about 9 inches (23 cm) long

Canola oil

4 tbsp (56 g) unsalted butter, melted, divided

1¼ cups (134 g) shredded mozzarella cheese

2 large tomatoes (about ¾ lb [340 g]), thinly sliced

¼ tsp kosher salt

¼ tsp red pepper flakes

3 oz (85 g) prosciutto, torn into bite-sized pieces

12 fresh basil leaves, torn into pieces

For the table: Pickled Red Onions (page 124) and Garlic Coeur à la Crème (page 128)

Heat the oven to 400°F (204°C).

On a lightly floured work surface, connect the two puff pastry sheets end-to-end by overlapping the ends by about ½ inch (1.3 cm) and pressing the ends together until the seam is secure. Both sheets combined should be about 18 inches (46 cm) long and should fit in the length of the sheet pan. If the puff pastry is too long for your sheet pan, remove the excessive dough so it can fit. If the puff pastry comes in one long sheet, disregard this step.

Spray a large sheet pan with canola oil and place the puff pastry onto the sheet pan. Brush with some of the melted butter.

Evenly distribute the mozzarella on top of the puff pastry, leaving about ½ inch (1.3 cm) of the perimeter of the puff pastry uncovered. Add the tomato slices and brush each tomato with some of the melted butter. Continue to brush the melted butter around the uncovered perimeter of the puff pastry. Evenly distribute the salt and red pepper flakes on top of the tomatoes and cheese. Place the sheet pan into the oven and cook for 32 to 40 minutes, or until the puff pastry is browned and the bottom is cooked.

Remove the tart from the oven and top with the prosciutto and basil. Slice and serve warm.

Pan-Seared Lamb Chops with Shallots and Mushrooms

A satisfying one-pan meal, Pan-Seared Lamb Chops with Shallots and Mushrooms is an elegant, simple dinner. This recipe combines the most basic of ingredients—oil, herbs, meat and wine—and the result is layers of flavor. The oil used to cook the lamb is infused with shallots and rosemary, while the pan is deglazed with white wine. A quick simmer and a touch of butter yields a splendid sauce.

Cooking Notes:

· *While Frenched lamb rib chops are artistic, I prefer lamb loin chops. This cut yields more meat due to the absence of the bone.*

· *When cooking lamb on medium-high heat for a long period, the fat can burn. Keep a watchful eye when searing and adjust the heat if the lamb begins to burn; look for blackened bits stuck to the pan or an off-putting scent. If this happens, remove the pan from the heat and add a bit of water to quickly deglaze.*

Yields 4–7 SERVINGS

1¼ tsp (8 g) kosher salt, divided

2 to 2½ lb (907 g to 1.1 kg) lamb loin chops

3 tbsp (45 ml) extra-virgin olive oil

8 to 10 shallots (¾ lb [340 g])

4 sprigs rosemary

12 oz (340 g) mushrooms, chopped

1 cup (240 ml) dry white wine

1 tbsp (14 g) unsalted butter

For the table: Herbed Crème Fraiche (page 123), Pickled Red Onions (page 124) and Browned Butter Toast (page 120)

Evenly distribute 1 teaspoon of the salt on both sides of the lamb chops and set aside. In a large skillet, add the oil, shallots and rosemary. Cook over medium heat for 5 minutes. Remove the shallots and rosemary and place onto a serving platter. Increase the heat to medium-high and allow the pan to heat for about 30 seconds.

Cooking in two batches, add half of the lamb to the skillet. Sear the lamb for 3 minutes per side, a total of 6 minutes, for medium-rare. For medium lamb chops, sear for 4 minutes per side, a total of 8 minutes. Remove the lamb and place onto the platter. Repeat this step with the remaining lamb.

Immediately remove the pan from the heat and add the mushrooms. Stir to coat with the fat and scrape up all of the browned bits stuck to the pan, which will be a lot. Don't worry. The mushrooms will release liquid as they cook, and this liquid will help to deglaze the pan. Continue to cook the mushrooms off the heat for 1 minute, stirring frequently.

Reduce the heat to medium and place the skillet back onto the cooktop. Return the shallots and rosemary to the skillet and cook for 1 to 2 minutes. Deglaze the pan with the wine. Simmer for 3 to 4 minutes, or until the liquid is slightly reduced. Add the butter and stir to incorporate. Pour the sauce over the lamb chops. Serve warm.

Baked Tarragon Lamb Meatballs

Do not be deceived by tarragon's delicate appearance. This lightweight herb has a strong flavor that pairs well with proteins. While this recipe showcases the unique flavor of tarragon, the mayonnaise brings a creamy touch of salt and umami that creates a very balanced meatball. These delightful baked meatballs are simple to assemble, quick to bake and are freezer friendly. Rejoice!

Cooking Notes:

- *If you do not have access to ground lamb, use ground beef, pork or turkey. Cooking time will vary depending on the protein used, so adjust accordingly.*

- *If the mayonnaise used is extra salty, reduce the amount of salt. If you do not have access to tarragon, try using fresh mint or basil.*

- *This recipe can be easily doubled to make 28 meatballs. If you double the recipe, do not double the amount of salt. Instead, just use an additional ¼ to ½ teaspoon.*

Yields 14 MEATBALLS

1½ lb (680 g) ground lamb

¼ tsp red pepper flakes (optional)

¾ tsp granulated garlic

¾ tsp kosher salt

3 tsp (13 g) mayonnaise

4 tsp (6 g) panko breadcrumbs

1 egg

⅓ cup (4 g) tarragon, chopped

For the table: Smothered Tomatoes (page 127), Pickled Red Onions (page 124) and Coconut Mushroom Gravy (page 131)

Heat the oven to 400°F (204°C). Line a rimmed sheet pan with parchment paper. Set aside.

In a large bowl, thoroughly combine the lamb, red pepper flakes (if using), garlic, salt, mayonnaise, breadcrumbs, egg and tarragon.

Using a 2-inch (5-cm) wide ice cream scoop, scoop out the meatballs. Place onto the parchment-lined rimmed sheet pan. Cook for 25 minutes, or until the lamb reaches the desired doneness. Remove the meatballs from the oven and cool for 5 minutes.

Serve warm with Baked Gorgonzola Polenta (page 101) or Rosemary Garlic Sour Cream Mashed Potatoes (page 114).

Braised Lamb Shoulder with Orzo

In this one-pan meal, lamb and orzo are brought together in a creamy, peppery sauce, creating a rustic and noteworthy dinner. Braised Lamb Shoulder with Orzo checks all the logistical boxes for a weeknight meal with its minimal prep work and ease of cooking. I find myself craving a large, warm bowl of comforting lamb and orzo during all seasons of the year.

Cooking Notes:

· *To ensure even cooking, cut the lamb into uniform pieces and be sure to thoroughly pat the lamb dry prior to browning. If the pan being used is wide enough to comfortably hold the entire amount of lamb without crowding, you can brown the lamb in one step.*

Yields 4–6 SERVINGS

1½ lb (680 g) boneless lamb shoulder, cut into 1-inch (2.5-cm) cubes

1 tsp kosher salt

½ to 1 tsp black pepper (depending on preference)

2 tbsp (30 ml) extra-virgin olive oil

1 cup (160 g) diced yellow onion

2 cups (480 ml) dry white wine

½ tsp dried oregano

4 cups (960 ml) low-sodium beef stock, divided

1¼ cups (233 g) uncooked orzo

For the table: Browned Butter Toast (page 120) and Pickled Red Onions (page 124)

Pat the lamb pieces dry. Salt and pepper the lamb and set aside.

Warm the oil in a large Dutch oven over high heat. Once hot, 3 to 4 minutes, add half of the lamb to the pan. Cook for a total of 6 to 8 minutes, turning the meat once or twice to brown all sides. Remove the lamb from the pan and repeat with the second batch. Once all the lamb is browned, lower the heat to medium and remove the pan from the heat.

Add the onion to the pan and stir to coat. Place the pan back onto the heat and cook for 3 minutes, stirring frequently. Deglaze the pan with the wine. Add the oregano and 3 cups (720 ml) of the stock and stir. Place the lamb pieces back into the pan and stir. Bring to a boil and then reduce the heat to low. Cover and simmer for 45 minutes to 1 hour.

After 45 minutes of simmering, check the lamb for tenderness. If it is easily pierced with a fork, add the orzo and 1 cup (240 ml) of the stock to the pan. Stir to combine. If the lamb is not tender, continue to cook for an additional 15 minutes or until tender. Once the orzo is added, continue to simmer until the sauce is thickened and the orzo is cooked all the way, about 15 minutes. Spoon the lamb and orzo into warm bowls. Serve immediately.

To add extra flavor, *serve with a squeeze of lemon juice.*

simple seafood

Seafood is a glorious ingredient. In addition to being filling, nutritious and unique in flavor profiles, it's quick to cook. When there is a combination of nutrition, taste and speediness, what's not to love?

These recipes showcase time-saving tips and utilize specific cooking methods to minimize the amount of cooking equipment needed and ingredients used. Three of these five recipes yield an entire meal in one recipe, making them great options for weekdays. The Broiled Lemon Salmon with Green Apple and Pine Nut Salad (page 50) is a happy meal and one that I enjoy making for its bright pops of color and tangy green apple flavor. Chili-Garlic Coconut Red Snapper with Broccolini and Peppers (page 58) is fragrant and filling, one of my weeknight favorites.

Creamy Shrimp with Garlic and Dill (page 57) is fast and can stand on its own as a meal, but can also be served on top of pasta or with Skillet Beef Tenderloin with Garlic Broccolini (page 33) for a bit of surf and turf. Another hybrid of land and sea is Duck Fat– Seared Scallops (page 53). It is fancy, quick to prep and easy to cook. My favorite element of this dish might be the duck fat breadcrumbs that top each seared scallop.

With seafood, quick meals can be assembled and served in under 30 minutes. And even more importantly, flavors and textures abound, which will not only please diner's palates but will also expand your kitchen skill set.

Broiled Lemon Salmon with Green Apple and Pine Nut Salad

When I think about this dish, I get excited. The warm, broiled lemon salmon served alongside a cold and tangy green apple salad is striking. From creamy to savory to tart to salty—the flavor components in this dish create an unforgettable and smartly constructed meal. With its minimal cook time and varying flavors, this wholesome and simple meal will become a new favorite.

Cooking Notes:

· *This can be made with a whole salmon fillet or six 6-ounce (170-g) salmon portions. If using a large fillet of salmon, ask a fishmonger for the most even cut (in thickness). There are many salmon pieces that are thin on one side and very thick on the other.*

· *You may not use all the mayonnaise called for in this recipe. That's okay. Use what is needed to coat the salmon and discard the rest.*

Yields 6 SERVINGS

¾ cup (96 g) pine nuts

3 lemons (zest of 3 and juice of 1, divided)

½ tsp kosher salt

3 tbsp (39 g) mayonnaise

2 lb (907 g) salmon

4 cups (420 g) green apples, diced into ¼- to ½-inch (6-mm to 1.3-cm) pieces

For the table: Herbed Crème Fraiche (page 123) and Pickled Red Onions (page 124)

Toast the pine nuts in a small skillet over low heat for 5 minutes or until golden and fragrant. Keep a watchful eye on them as you toast—if the heat is too hot, they can easily burn. Once toasted, remove the pine nuts from the skillet; they will continue to cook and potentially burn if left in the pan. Set aside.

Adjust the oven rack to 6 inches (15 cm) below the broiler. Heat the broiler to 500°F (260°C).

Evenly distribute the lemon zest, salt and mayonnaise onto each salmon fillet. The amount of mayonnaise varies depending upon the size of the salmon. Use what is needed and discard the rest.

Place the salmon into the oven and broil for 7 to 9 minutes or until the salmon reaches an internal temperature of 135°F (57°C). This time will vary depending upon the thickness of the salmon fillet. Remove the salmon from the oven and set aside. The internal temperature of the salmon will increase a few degrees once removed from the oven. Top the fish with juice from half the lemon. Let cool for 5 to 10 minutes.

While the fish is cooling, toss the green apples with the toasted pine nuts and juice from half the lemon.

Place the apple salad onto serving plates and top with salmon slices. Serve immediately.

Duck Fat–Seared Scallops

Scallops can instantly elevate a dining experience, and pairing scallops with duck fat will make anyone sharing your table feel extra special. This dish is simple in preparation and minimal in cook time. A quick sear in the skillet makes for an easy and delicious weeknight entrée. Pair this simple seafood with a quick-cooking side, like Herbes de Provence Couscous with Buttermilk (page 97), and dinner will be done in a delightful flash.

Cooking Notes:

- *1½ pounds (680 g) will yield 12 to 14 scallops. To create the best possible sear, it is critical to pat the scallops dry and to have a hot, evenly heated skillet.*

- *Jarred duck fat can be found at some high-end grocers or specialty food stores.*

- *The finishing touch of fresh thyme or lemon zest can change the entire flavor landscape of this dish. I find that fresh thyme creates more of a fall and winter feel, whereas lemon zest can feel more like spring and summer. Of course, you can combine the two and have the best of all seasons. If neither seem appealing, choose what seems the most intriguing; dill, chives or even celery leaves are good options.*

Yields 4 SERVINGS

1½ lb (680 g) large scallops

½ tsp kosher salt, plus more for finishing

3 tbsp (36 g) duck fat

2 large shallots, halved

½ cup (37 g) panko breadcrumbs

½ tsp fresh thyme, chopped, or zest of 2 lemons

For the table: Herbed Crème Fraiche (page 123)

Using paper towels, pat the scallops dry and evenly distribute the salt on all sides. Set aside.

Place the duck fat and shallots into a flat-bottomed skillet. Warm over high heat. Once the pan is hot, about 4 minutes, remove the shallots and set aside. Add the scallops and cook for 2½ to 3 minutes per side, basting the tops of the scallops with the duck fat while sautéing. Cook for a total of 5 to 6 minutes. The duck fat will eventually brown, and it is okay if this begins to happen during the cooking process. Browned food imparts flavor. It is when the brown goes to black that issues arise.

Remove the pan from the heat and reduce the heat to low. Place the scallops onto a serving plate and set aside.

Add the breadcrumbs to the skillet. Stir to coat. Return the skillet to the heat and toast until browned, 1 to 2 minutes.

Top the scallops with the duck fat breadcrumbs and thyme. Salt to taste.

Roasted Orange Barramundi with Sourdough Croutons and Basil

There are many components to love in this meal, and I can't pick just one favorite ingredient. After first settling on the croutons as my favorite, I felt disloyal to the orange-roasted barramundi and vacillated once again. This just goes to show that all parts of this simple yet sophisticated dish are standouts and well deserving of praise.

Cooking Notes:

- *The cook time for the fish will depend upon the thickness. If you cannot find barramundi, ask the fishmonger for a similar white fish to substitute.*

- *To ensure delicious croutons, select a quality sourdough from a trusted bakery. Be sure to include the basil with the crouton mixture—it really livens the dish.*

- *Resist the urge to cook the barramundi on the croutons. While it would be ideal to only cook with one sheet pan, this separation of the two ingredients allows the croutons to become golden and crunchy.*

Yields 4–6 SERVINGS

3 barramundi fillets (about 2 lb [907 g])

1 tbsp (15 ml) extra-virgin olive oil

¾ tsp kosher salt

4 oranges (zest of 3 and 1 thinly sliced)

6 cups (250 g) sourdough bread, crust removed and cut into bite-sized pieces

4 tbsp (56 g) unsalted butter, melted

½ cup (5 g) fresh basil leaves, chopped

For the table: Pickled Red Onions (page 124) and Herbed Crème Fraiche (page 123)

Adjust the oven racks to accommodate two sheet pans. Line two rimmed sheet pans with foil. Set aside.

Heat the oven to 425°F (218°C).

Place the barramundi fillets onto one sheet pan. Evenly distribute the oil, salt, orange zest and slices onto the 3 fillets. Set aside.

Place the sourdough pieces into a bowl and toss with the melted butter. Place the buttered sourdough onto the second sheet pan and roast in the oven for 8 minutes.

After 8 minutes, toss the croutons and place them back in the oven, adding the sheet pan with the barramundi. Cook until the fish reaches an internal temperature of 145°F (63°C), 10 to 13 minutes. Remove the fish and croutons from the oven.

Stir the croutons and let cool for 5 minutes. Place the croutons back into their original bowl and toss with the basil. Serve the barramundi warm with the croutons and basil.

Creamy Shrimp with Garlic and Dill

An array of great meals can be created from this one simple, filling and quick-cooking recipe. Creamy Shrimp with Garlic and Dill is delicious served with pasta, rice, mashed potatoes, crusty bread—or even eaten alone. Be sure to add the fresh dill—it is not the same without it. This tangy herb pairs wonderfully with the cream and shrimp and adds a bright, sweet and sour element to the dish.

Cooking Notes:

- *Be sure to purchase shrimp with the tails on. Utilizing the tails to infuse the cream enhances the sauce.*

- *If you have a half-used bottle of dry white wine, you can substitute it for the water to add additional flavor. If fresh dill is unavailable, use tarragon or basil.*

- *This recipe is salt forward, so I recommend serving it with a starchy pasta or rice. The salt can easily be reduced to ¼ teaspoon if you prefer.*

Yields 4–6 SERVINGS

1½ lb (680 g) peeled and deveined shrimp, tail on

½ tsp kosher salt, divided

1 cup (240 ml) heavy cream

2 tbsp (28 g) unsalted butter

5 cloves garlic, chopped

½ cup (120 ml) water

¼ cup (60 ml) cognac

1 tsp white wine vinegar

2 tbsp (2 g) fresh dill, chopped

For the table: Garlic Coeur à la Crème (page 128) and Browned Butter Toast (page 120)

Remove the shrimp tails and place the tails into a small saucepan. Set aside. Place the shrimp into a bowl and sprinkle with ¼ teaspoon of the salt. Stir well and set aside.

Pour the cream into the saucepan with the shrimp tails. Simmer the cream over low heat for 15 minutes. Into a small bowl, strain the cream from the tails and set aside.

In a flat-bottomed skillet, add the butter and warm over medium heat. Once the butter is melted, add the garlic and cook until fragrant, 30 seconds to 1 minute. Increase the heat to medium-high and add the water and cognac. Let the liquid simmer until it is reduced by half, 2 to 3 minutes.

Add the strained cream, shrimp and ¼ teaspoon of the salt to the skillet. Stir well. Reduce the heat and continue cook for 4 to 6 minutes, or until all the shrimp is cooked.

Remove from the heat and stir in the vinegar and dill. Serve warm, at room temperature or chilled.

To add extra flavor, *thinly slice 2 Roma tomatoes and add to the cream mixture to simmer with the shrimp.*

Chili-Garlic Coconut Red Snapper with Broccolini and Peppers

Chili-garlic sauce is a premade Asian condiment that can be found in most grocery stores. It contains chopped chiles and ample amounts of garlic. This flavorful condiment is an easy and quick marinade for a variety of ingredients, from fish to vegetables. For this meal, spicy chili-garlic sauce and creamy coconut milk are combined to create a luxuriously heat-filled topping that complements both the red snapper and the broccolini. Jasmine rice is the perfect companion to this dish. If there are leftovers, chilled snapper is delicious on a bed of crisp arugula for a light lunch or dinner.

Cooking Notes:

- *This recipe can easily be halved. Cook only one fillet and use half of the ingredients for the foil packets. Keep the sauce ingredients the same, as you will probably want to pour it on everything. If you want to make extra sauce, double the sauce ingredients—except the salt, which should be added to taste at the end of cooking.*

Yields 6–8 SERVINGS

1 (13.6-oz [402-ml]) can of coconut milk

½ tsp ground ginger

¾ tsp kosher salt, divided

1 tsp sugar

1 tsp white wine vinegar

3 tbsp (45 ml) chili-garlic sauce, divided

1 bell pepper, seeded, cored and sliced

2 lb (907 g) red snapper (2 fillets, about 1 lb [454 g] each)

1 lb (454 g) broccolini, divided

2 tsp (10 ml) canola oil, divided

Heat the oven to 500°F (260°C).

In a saucepan, combine the coconut milk, ginger, ¼ teaspoon of the salt, the sugar, vinegar, 1 tablespoon (15 ml) of the chili-garlic sauce and the bell pepper. Cook over low heat for 15 minutes, stirring occasionally.

Using two large sheets of foil, place one snapper fillet and ½ pound of broccolini onto each sheet. The broccolini should be on one half of the foil, and the fillet should be on the other. Evenly distribute the oil and ½ teaspoon of the salt onto the fillets and broccolini. Depending on the amount of heat preferred, smear 2 to 3 teaspoons (10 to 15 ml) of chili-garlic sauce on top of each snapper fillet, covering the entire top.

Pull up the sides of the foil to create a packet (do not seal yet). Inside each foil packet, top the fillets with 2 tablespoons (30 ml) of the coconut chili-garlic liquid. Seal the packets, place onto a rimmed sheet pan and cook for 15 to 18 minutes, or until the fish reaches an internal temperature of 145°F (63°C).

Remove the sheet pan from the oven. Slice the fish into individual servings and serve with the broccolini topped with the coconut chili-garlic sauce.

To add extra flavor, *top with lime wedges and basil.*

comforting classics

Bringing comfort food to a dinner table makes for pleasant, memorable mealtimes. While the term "comfort food" often means an excess of unhealthy ingredients or cooking methods, this section is dedicated to changing that perception. These recipes show how to transform wholesome—albeit rich—ingredients into cozy, satisfying meals while maintaining balance.

Instead of being fried, chicken thighs are gently browned in butter then braised in the oven with cream and spinach. Onions are caramelized and browned before being added to a pan of braising beef in an herbed stock. Dried black beans are combined with a bell pepper—infused chicken stock and then quickly pressure cooked.

Most of these recipes require only one or two cooking pans and use minimal ingredients. This type of cooking is easy to pull off and is oh-so-pleasing.

While the beloved butter and cheese are frequently used, like in the Chicken and Spinach Gratin (page 65), some recipes are dairy free, like the Pressure-Cooked Cuban Black Bean Soup (page 73). Some of these recipes are fitting for weeknight meals for their quickness in preparation and cook time, like the Gnocchi with Browned Butter, Peas and Prosciutto (page 62) and Harissa Baked Eggs with Goat Cheese (page 70). If time is handy, Eggplant Parmesan (page 77) and French Onion Beef Stew (page 78) are worthwhile endeavors that will leave leftovers for the following day. Porcini Beef Ragù (page 69) is a dish that stole my heart from the moment of its creation. It uses ground dried porcini to season the browned beef. The result is a ragù full of umami—without a mushroom texture. It can be used in a variety of dishes—pasta! Crostini! Pizza!

Cozy dinners of homemade comfort food are food hugs that resonate throughout a lifetime. Enjoy these moments and repeat often.

Gnocchi with Browned Butter, Peas and Prosciutto

Gnocchi is a quick-cooking dumpling that makes for a filling and hassle-free meal. A luxurious browned butter–red wine vinegar sauce pairs well with the flavors of the prosciutto, Parmesan and basil. This is a simple and savory meal that requires minimal prep and cook time.

Cooking Notes:

- *Either fresh or frozen peas will work in this recipe. The cook time will vary depending on the peas used.*

- *Prosciutto is easiest to cut when cold, so make sure it is not at room temperature. To cut, stack all the prosciutto and make thin vertical slices, then thin horizontal cuts along the slices. Use your fingers to gently toss the prosciutto to untangle the small shreds.*

Yields 4 SERVINGS

¾ cup (103 g) frozen peas

1½ lb (680 g) gnocchi

5 tbsp (70 g) unsalted butter

1 tbsp (15 ml) red wine vinegar

3 oz (85 g) prosciutto, chilled and finely chopped

20 fresh basil leaves, finely chopped

¹/₃ cup (38 g) freshly grated Parmesan

For the table: Browned Butter Toast (page 120) and Smothered Tomatoes (page 127)

Fill a medium-sized pan with water and bring to a boil. Place the peas into the water and cook, 5 to 6 minutes. Using a slotted spoon, remove the peas and set aside. Reserve the boiling water to cook the gnocchi. Place the gnocchi into the boiling water and cook until the gnocchi begin to rise to the surface, 4 to 5 minutes.

Meanwhile, melt the butter in a skillet set over medium heat until browned, 10 to 15 minutes. Increase the heat to high and add the vinegar. Let the mixture simmer for 30 seconds. Remove from the heat and swirl the pan, then set aside until the gnocchi is finished cooking.

Place the cooked gnocchi into the browned butter mixture and return the skillet to the cooktop. Cook over medium heat, tossing the gnocchi occasionally, for 4 minutes or until lightly browned. Repeat this step if the pan cannot hold all the gnocchi.

With a slotted spoon, scoop out half the gnocchi and place onto a serving platter. A large gratin dish works well. Top with half the peas, prosciutto and fresh basil. Repeat this step to create a second layer. Drizzle the remaining browned butter over the top layer of gnocchi and top with the Parmesan. Serve immediately.

Chicken and Spinach Gratin

A pièce de résistance, this recipe combines two of my favorite ingredients for gratins: chicken and spinach. This fancy-sounding dish is easy to prepare, and the result is a meal suited for a casual weeknight dinner or a formal dinner party. Rich, savory flavors are created from the browned chicken skin, butter, Gruyère and cream. A hint of black pepper is an aromatic thread that ties the dish together.

Cooking Notes:

- *If you have a half-used bottle of dry white wine sitting in the fridge, feel free to use it to deglaze the pan instead of water.*

- *To prevent the gratin from being watery, be sure to squeeze out as much liquid from the spinach as possible.*

- *Chicken thighs often have an excess amount of skin. I suggest removing some of the skin before cooking.*

Yields 6–8 SERVINGS

2 (16-oz [454-g]) bags frozen chopped spinach

1¼ tsp (8 g) kosher salt, divided

6 to 8 chicken thighs (3 lb [1.4 kg])

2 tbsp (28 g) unsalted butter, divided

1½ cups (240 g) finely diced yellow onion

½ cup (120 ml) water

½ tsp black pepper

½ tsp white wine vinegar

½ cup (120 ml) cream

1 cup (108 g) Gruyère, grated

For the table: Browned Butter Toast (page 120)

Heat the oven to 400°F (204°C).

Fill a large pot with water and bring to a boil. Cook the spinach in the water for 2 minutes. Drain and put the spinach into a mesh strainer placed over a bowl. This will allow the excess water to drip out while you prepare the chicken. Press the spinach with the back of a wooden spoon to help the process along.

Meanwhile, salt the chicken thighs—including under the skin—with 1 teaspoon of the salt and set aside. For tips on salting chicken under the skin, see the cooking notes for the Rosemary-Orange Spatchcock Chicken (page 12).

Select a large braising pan or Dutch oven that can hold 6 to 8 thighs and 2 pounds (907 g) of spinach. Melt the butter over medium heat. Once the butter is melted, place the chicken into the pan and cook for 20 minutes, turning every 5 minutes. Remove the chicken and set aside. Place the onion into the pan and cook until softened, about 4 minutes.

Deglaze the pan with the water. Stir in the pepper, vinegar, cream, Gruyère, spinach and ¼ teaspoon of the salt. Stir to combine. Nestle the chicken and its juices into the spinach mixture. Place into the oven and cook for 20 to 25 minutes, or until the chicken reaches an internal temperature of 165°F (74°C). Remove from the oven and serve warm.

Chorizo Baked Beans

With only one item to chop (onions), the prep for Chorizo Baked Beans is a breeze. Deep flavors are created with just a few ingredients: chorizo, browned tomato paste and brown sugar. The time spent simmering in the oven creates a rich, concentrated chorizo sauce that becomes a perfect partner for the beans. Since the overall flavor of this recipe is influenced by the chorizo, it is important to select a chorizo that you enjoy. Leftovers pair well the next morning with biscuits and runny eggs.

Cooking Notes:

- *This recipe will work with either raw or precooked chorizo, but raw works best as it does not dry out.*

Yields 6–8 SERVINGS

1 tsp extra-virgin olive oil

6 to 8 raw chorizo links (24 oz [680 g])

1 cup (160 g) diced yellow onion

4 tbsp (64 g) tomato paste

2 cups (480 ml) water

1½ tsp (9 g) kosher salt

1 tbsp (15 ml) white wine vinegar

½ cup (105 g) brown sugar

3 (15.5-oz [439-g]) cans pinto beans, drained and rinsed

For the table: Browned Butter Toast (page 120) and Pickled Red Onions (page 124)

Heat the oven to 375°F (191°C).

In a large skillet, add the oil and warm over medium-high heat, 2 to 3 minutes. Add the chorizo links and cook, 2 minutes per side. Lower the heat to medium and remove the skillet from the heat. Reserve 1 teaspoon of any rendered fat in the skillet and discard the rest. Add the onion to the skillet and stir to combine. Return to the heat and cook for 2 minutes, stirring occasionally.

Add the tomato paste and cook until browned, 1 to 2 minutes. Stir frequently to prevent burning. Deglaze the pan with the water, scraping up any bits stuck to the bottom. Add the salt, vinegar and brown sugar to the liquid. Add the beans and stir to combine. Increase the heat to high and bring to a boil. Reduce heat to medium and simmer for 5 minutes, stirring occasionally. Add the chorizo back into the pan and place into the oven. Cook for 45 minutes to 1 hour, or until the cooking liquid has thickened.

Remove from the oven and serve warm.

To add extra flavor, *top with cilantro.*

Porcini Beef Ragù

A hearty, rich and satisfying ragù can be a weeknight reality with this Porcini Beef Ragù. The sauce is ready in under 45 minutes, and it is unmatched in flavor due to one unique ingredient: dried porcini mushrooms. If you are a fan of mushroom flavor but do not like the texture, this recipe is for you. The ground porcini produces mushroom essence without the infamous texture. If there are any leftovers—which is rarely the case—they can be frozen. I recommend doubling the recipe.

Cooking Notes:

- *Before grinding the dried porcini, be sure to tear up any large chunks. Depending on the size of the food processor or coffee grinder, you may have to blitz the porcini in batches. When grinding the porcini, be sure to use a grinder you have designated specifically for spices. A grinder used for coffee beans will make the porcini taste like coffee.*

- *The concentrated flavor for this ragù comes from the browning of the onion, ground beef and tomato paste. Be sure to get a good brown during each stage to ensure maximum flavor.*

Yields 4–6 SERVINGS

½ oz (14 g) dried porcini

1 medium yellow onion, peeled and quartered

2 tbsp (30 ml) extra-virgin olive oil

1¼ tsp (8 g) kosher salt, divided

1½ lb (680 g) ground beef

2 tbsp (32 g) tomato paste

2 cups (480 ml) water, plus more as needed

1 cup (90 g) grated Parmesan, plus more for topping

For the table: Browned Butter Toast (page 120)

In a small food processor or coffee grinder, grind the porcini until granulated. Set aside and wipe the food processor clean. Place the onion into the food processor and blitz until pureed.

In a large flat-bottomed skillet, add the oil and warm over medium-high heat. Add the onion and ½ teaspoon of the salt. Cook until browned, 8 to 12 minutes, stirring occasionally.

Add the ground beef and ¾ teaspoon of the salt. Cook until browned and sticking to the pan, 9 to 15 minutes. Stir often. If you are ambitious with the heat (like me) and the bottom of the pan looks as if it could go from brown to black, add a smidge of water to quickly deglaze. Resume browning.

Add the tomato paste and cook for 1 to 2 minutes, stirring occasionally to prevent burning. Deglaze the pan with the 2 cups (480 ml) of water. Add the ground porcini and stir. Bring to a boil, then reduce the heat to low and simmer. Cook for 20 minutes, stirring occasionally.

Add the Parmesan and stir to combine. If the sauce begins to look too thick, add more water and continue to simmer to the desired consistency.

Serve topped with freshly grated Parmesan. The ragù pairs well with pasta or polenta.

Harissa Baked Eggs with Goat Cheese

This dish is satisfying for any meal of the day. Cooking the eggs with butter, cream and harissa elevates the eggs beyond the more traditional boiled or scrambled preparation. The fresh garlic and goat cheese complement the harissa and make the dish feel like a special occasion meal. When baked in a unique dish—I like to use a shallow ribbed-edge tart pan—the eggs become a charming centerpiece for the table.

Cooking Notes:

- *If serving this for breakfast, serve with bacon; for lunch and dinner, serve with a green salad. No matter when you eat this dish, always serve crusty bread.*

- *If you do not have cream, half-and-half or whole milk will do just fine.*

- *This recipe calls for harissa sauce, not the traditional North African harissa paste, which tends to be more concentrated and salty. Most grocery stores carry harissa sauce.*

Yields 4–6 SERVINGS

6 large eggs

¾ cup (207 g) mild harissa sauce

2 tbsp (30 ml) heavy whipping cream

2 tbsp (28 g) unsalted butter, sliced into 6 pieces

4 cloves garlic, chopped, divided

¼ cup (31 g) crumbled goat cheese, plus more to top, divided

¼ tsp kosher salt, divided

For the table: Browned Butter Toast (page 120)

Adjust the oven rack to about 6 inches (15 cm) from the broiler. Heat the broiler to 550°F (288°C). If the broiler does not go to 550°F (288°C), the cook time may be slightly longer for both stages of the cooking process.

Crack the eggs into a bowl and set aside. In a 9-inch (23-cm) ceramic tart pan, add the harissa and cream. Stir to combine. Place the pieces of butter evenly throughout the harissa cream mixture. Place the pan into the oven and broil for 4 to 5 minutes, or until the harissa starts to boil and the butter begins to brown.

Remove the pan from the oven and add half of the chopped garlic, half of the goat cheese and half of the salt. Stir well to combine. Gently pour the eggs into the pan, ensuring they are evenly spaced. Evenly distribute the remaining salt, garlic and goat cheese on top of the harissa and eggs. Place back into the oven.

Broil for 5½ to 7 minutes (5½ minutes for runny yolks, 7 minutes for firm yolks), remove from the oven and let sit for 1 minute. When broiling, the transition from browned to burnt is quick. Keep a watchful eye. Serve with crusty bread.

To add extra flavor, *top with herbs like fresh basil, cilantro, dill and/or mint.*

Pressure-Cooked Cuban Black Bean Soup

Large batch cooking—when used with the right recipes—can create many wonderful, satisfying meals. This is a simple, wholesome recipe that I often make solely to put in the freezer. While this recipe is titled "soup," it has the ability to be much more. The beans can be strained from the cooking liquid and used for tacos, or pureed to make a dip or a side dish. Pico de gallo, fresh cilantro and tortilla chips are just a few of the many toppings that can liven the soup.

Cooking Notes:

- *I have found that there are particular ingredients that do extremely well in the electric pressure cooker. Beans fall into this category. If soaked overnight, beans can cook relatively quickly—about 45 minutes once all is said and done. If you do not have an electric pressure cooker or prefer a long cooktop simmer, this recipe is easily adjustable. Sauté the onion and peppers in a large pan on the cooktop and simmer with a bit more cooking liquid than listed. Slowly simmer the beans until you reach your desired tenderness.*

- *Cooked either way, this soup freezes well for 3 to 4 months. If the beans are not soaked, pressure cook on high for 30 minutes with a 20-minute natural pressure release.*

Yields 12 SERVINGS

1 tbsp (15 ml) canola oil

½ cup (80 g) diced yellow onion

2 green bell peppers (about ½ lb [227 g]), 1 seeded and diced, 1 cored and halved

2 tsp (12 g) kosher salt, divided, plus more to taste

1 lb (454 g) dried black beans, soaked overnight

6 cups (1.4 L) low-sodium chicken stock

½ tsp dried oregano

1 tbsp plus 2 tsp (12 g) ground cumin

1 tbsp (15 ml) red wine vinegar

For the table: Pickled Red Onions (page 124)

Add the oil, onion, bell peppers and ½ teaspoon of the salt to the pressure cooker insert. Using the sauté feature, cook for 4 minutes, stirring occasionally. Add the beans and stir to coat. Add the stock, oregano, cumin and 1½ teaspoon (9 g) of the salt to the beans and stir well. Secure the lid on the pressure cooker and cook on high pressure for 7 minutes. If overcooked beans are preferred, pressure cook for 9 minutes.

Turn off the pressure cooker and allow the pressure to release naturally for 10 to 15 minutes, then manually release any remaining pressure. Remove the lid, then stir in the vinegar and salt to taste. If desired, serve topped with sour cream.

One-Pan Lemon Parmesan Linguine

This decadent One-Pan Lemon Parmesan Linguine is quick to cook and quick to please. The recipe uses all parts of the lemon to really make the pasta shine.

Cooking Notes:

- *This recipe is lemon forward. The amount of juice extracted from the lemons depends on their size. I use medium-sized, ripe lemons and I get an ample amount of juice. Use a mesh strainer to ensure the seeds are separated from the juice.*

- *The sauce will appear to have too much liquid at first, but the rest time will help it to thicken.*

Yields 6–8 SERVINGS

4 lemons

3 tbsp (42 g) unsalted butter, divided

6 cloves garlic, chopped

6 cups (1.4 L) water

¼ tsp ground pepper, plus more to taste

1 tsp kosher salt, plus more to taste

1 lb (454 g) linguine

¾ cup (180 ml) heavy cream

1 cup (114 g) finely grated Parmesan

For the table: Smothered Tomatoes (page 127)

Remove the peel from one of the lemons, creating three strips of peel. Repeat with a second lemon. Zest the 2 remaining lemons. Juice 2 to 3 lemons, depending on the size of the lemons and the desired tartness. In a large pan, melt 2 tablespoons (28 g) of the butter over medium heat. Add the garlic and cook until fragrant, about 1 minute. Add the water, lemon strips, pepper, salt and linguine. Increase the heat to high and bring to a boil. Don't worry if the pasta does not initially fit inside the pan. While the water comes to a boil, the linguine will soften and relax into the cooking liquid. This will take 4 to 5 minutes. You may need to push the noodles into the pan until they are submerged.

Once the water is boiling, reduce the heat to medium-high to create a gentle boil and cook the pasta for 7 minutes, stirring occasionally to prevent sticking. Add the cream. Reduce the heat to medium and continue to cook for 3 minutes, or until the sauce is thickened and the pasta is cooked to al dente. Stir frequently. Turn off the heat, stir in 1 tablespoon (14 g) of the butter and let melt. Add the lemon juice, lemon zest and Parmesan and stir to combine. Let cool for 5 to 8 minutes to allow the sauce to thicken.

Place into serving bowls and top with additional lemon zest, salt and pepper to taste.

To add extra flavor, *toss in chopped arugula and fresh basil.*

Eggplant Parmesan

Casserole-style Eggplant Parmesan takes me back to the summer I studied in Italy. While dining in a rustic trattoria in Tuscany, I stumbled across an Eggplant Parmesan unlike anything I had ever experienced stateside. This recipe is an homage to that life-altering moment when I ate a version of this dish that was not coated with breadcrumbs and fried. Instead, it tasted of fresh basil, eggplant, tomatoes and mozzarella. Every time I eat baked Eggplant Parmesan, I am instantly transported back to my twenties, living freely in a foreign country and happily discovering new life on every cobblestoned street. This meal is full of memories and tribute. Buon appetito!

Cooking Notes:

- *I recommend lining the sheet pans with foil before roasting the eggplant to make for an easy cleanup.*

- *When layering the roasted eggplant in the baking dish, I like to do three rows of four to five rounds. This will depend upon the size of the eggplant and the baking dish. Try not to use Japanese eggplant since they are significantly smaller, thinner and sweeter. It is critical to slice the eggplant as evenly as possible to ensure an even roast. If you cut ½-inch (1.3-cm)-thick rounds, expect to cook the eggplant a bit longer.*

- *If the cheese starts to brown while baking, cover the dish with foil.*

Yields 6 MAIN SERVINGS OR 8–10 SIDE SERVINGS

3 lb (1.4 kg) eggplant, sliced into ¼- to ½-inch (6-mm to 1.3-cm) thick rounds

¼ cup (60 ml) extra-virgin olive oil

1 tsp kosher salt, divided

1 (28-oz [794-g]) can crushed tomatoes

1 cup (110 g) grated Parmesan, plus more to top

2½ cups (260 g) grated mozzarella, divided

20 to 24 fresh basil leaves, plus more for topping, chopped

For the table: Browned Butter Toast (page 120)

Heat the oven to 425°F (218°C).

Place the eggplant rounds onto two rimmed sheet pans and evenly top with the olive oil and ½ teaspoon of the salt. Roast for 20 minutes. Remove from the oven and let cool slightly.

Add ½ teaspoon of the salt to the can of tomatoes and stir. Add ⅔ cup (161 g) of the tomatoes to the bottom of a large ceramic baking dish. Add one layer of eggplant rounds to the baking dish. Top with half of the Parmesan, ¾ cup (78 g) of the mozzarella and half of the basil leaves. Top with 1 cup (245 g) of the tomatoes. With the back of a spoon, evenly smooth the tomatoes to cover the entire top of the eggplant and cheese. Repeat with a final layer of eggplant, Parmesan, mozzarella, basil and tomatoes, using the same amount of each ingredient as the first layer. You'll have a small amount of crushed tomatoes left over, since using the entire can will lead to a soggy Eggplant Parmesan. Discard the leftover tomatoes or save to use later. Top with the remaining 1 cup (104 g) of the mozzarella.

Bake for 35 to 45 minutes, or until slightly browned on top and the eggplant is cooked all the way through. Remove and let cool for 10 to 15 minutes. Top with fresh torn basil and additional Parmesan. Serve warm.

French Onion Beef Stew

Traditional homemade French onion soup is a conundrum to me. The time needed to slice pounds of onions, to caramelize the onions and to simmer the soup can be daunting. Then, after all that hard work, what remains is a soup that—albeit rich and full of umami—isn't completely filling. Luckily, this recipe combines the richness of French onion soup with the heartiness of tender beef, creating a satisfying stew worthy of its time and effort.

Cooking Notes:

· Herb bouquets can typically be found in the produce department at your local market. If you can't find one, simply create your own.

· To channel the classic French onion soup, after the soup is cooked, heat the broiler to 500°F (260°C). Ladle the soup into bowls, top with baguette slices, sprinkle with Gruyère and broil until the cheese is slightly golden and melted.

Yields 4–6 SERVINGS

2 lb (907 g) beef stew meat, cut into 1½-inch (3.8-cm) cubes

4 tbsp (60 ml) olive oil, divided

6 cups (1.4 L) beef stock

1½ tsp (9 g) kosher salt, divided, plus more for finishing

½ tsp black pepper

1 bundle of an herb bouquet (basil, rosemary, bay leaf and thyme), securely tied with kitchen twine

6 cups (960 g) sliced yellow onions

½ cup (120 ml) cognac

2 tbsp (28 g) unsalted butter

Pat the beef dry and set aside. In a Dutch oven, add 1 tablespoon (15 ml) of the oil and warm over medium-high heat for 3 minutes. Working in two batches, place the beef into the pan and brown, about 5 minutes, turning occasionally to ensure browning on all sides. Remove from the pan. Repeat with the remaining beef.

Deglaze the pan with the stock and add the browned beef, 1 teaspoon of the salt, the pepper and herb bouquet to the cooking liquid. Bring to a boil and reduce to a simmer. Cover and cook on low for 2 to 2½ hours.

Once the cooking liquid starts simmering, begin to caramelize the onions. In a skillet, add 1 tablespoon (15 ml) of the oil and half of the onions. Top with ¼ teaspoon of the salt. Repeat this step to create a second layer of oil, onions and salt. Cook over medium-low heat for 45 minutes to 1 hour. Do not touch the onions for the first 20 to 25 minutes. After 20 to 25 minutes, begin stirring the onions occasionally to prevent burning. Once the onions are brown, deglaze the pan with the cognac and stir.

Add the caramelized onions and butter to the stew. There will be about 1 hour of cook time remaining once the onions are added to the simmering liquid. Continue to simmer until it reaches 2 to 2½ hours of total cook time. Once the beef is easily pierced with a fork and the sauce has thickened, remove from the heat. Salt to taste. Ladle into warm bowls and serve with crusty bread.

satisfying vegetables

Vegetables are versatile and filling; they can be an entire meal themselves. Rotating exciting meatless meals into a weekly dinner routine is a joy. In this chapter, all five recipes are filling enough to be a main course, and when paired with a leafy green salad or crusty bread, they prove to be as satisfying as a protein-focused meal. They can also be served as a side. The choice is up to you.

In this chapter, the delights of roasted vegetables abound. Roasted Brussels and Carrots with Tahini (page 89) is a one-pan wonder that utilizes high heat to roast the vegetables and achieve browned, golden goodness. Another simple, flavorful favorite is Harissa-Roasted Cabbage and Potatoes with Yogurt-Dill Sauce (page 82). It is a reliable weeknight meal that fuses the classic cabbage and potato combination with two mighty ingredients: harissa and dill. Spanish Pisto (page 90) is adaptable to meet lunch

and dinnertime needs. I not only use Spanish Pisto as a main dish, but also as a side, dip and even a topping for roasted meats. Lemon-Asparagus Baked Rice (page 85) infuses basmati rice with the subtle and earthy flavor of asparagus. Cauliflower Gratin (page 86), while fully cooked on the cooktop, benefits from time spent in the oven that helps to marry the cauliflower with ginger and cream, creating one of my most favorite meals.

Vegetables are more than just side dishes. They are main components that can enrich a table and be its focus. Embracing this fact is a welcomed change to any weekly meal rotation, expanding dinner horizons and cooking methods.

Harissa-Roasted Cabbage and Potatoes with Yogurt-Dill Sauce

This is an enticing meatless meal. The classic pairing of cabbage and potatoes is enhanced with the powerful flavors of harissa and tangy yogurt. While two sheet pans are used to ensure crispy potatoes, this meal still falls into the "one-pan wonder" category.

Cooking Notes:

- *Be sure to use harissa sauce (not paste) in this recipe. The amount of salt can vary with brands, so be sure to taste the harissa and adjust the salt as necessary.*

- *While it may be tempting to combine the cabbage and potatoes onto one sheet pan, please don't. The liquid the cabbage releases will prevent the potatoes from crisping.*

Yields 4 MAIN SERVINGS OR 8 SIDE SERVINGS

4 tbsp (60 ml) extra-virgin olive oil, divided

2 tsp (12 g) kosher salt, divided

1½ lb (680 g) small, round Yukon gold potatoes, halved

1 cup (256 g) mild harissa sauce

2 tbsp (30 ml) white wine vinegar, divided

1 head green cabbage (about 3 lb [1.4 kg]), sliced into wedges

1½ cups (387 g) plain yogurt

¼ cup (3 g) fresh dill, chopped, plus more for serving

Position one oven rack about 6 inches (15 cm) from the top of the oven and a second rack in the bottom third of the oven. Line two rimmed sheet pans with foil and set aside.

Heat the oven to 450°F (232°C).

In a large bowl, thoroughly combine 1 tablespoon (15 ml) of the oil and 1 teaspoon of the salt. Place the potatoes into the bowl and toss to coat. Using a slotted spoon, add the potatoes to one sheet pan.

In a bowl, combine the harissa, 1 tablespoon (15 ml) of the vinegar, 1 tablespoon (15 ml) of the oil and ¾ teaspoon of the salt. Place the cabbage onto the second sheet pan, being sure not to stack the wedges. Working with one cabbage wedge at a time, separate the wedge into halves. Add a smear of the harissa mixture to the top of the bottom half of the wedge. Return the top half to the wedge, sandwiching the harissa mixture between the two halves.

Repeat these steps for all the wedges. Drizzle the remaining harissa mixture on top of the cabbage. Drizzle 1 tablespoon (15 ml) of the oil over the parts of the cabbage not covered by the harissa. Cover the sheet pan with foil, sealing the sides well.

Place both sheet pans into the oven. Roast for 15 minutes. Reduce the heat to 425°F (218°C) and remove the foil cover from the cabbage. Stir the potatoes. Cook for an additional 25 to 30 minutes, or until the vegetables are browned.

While the vegetables are roasting, combine the yogurt, 1 tablespoon (15 ml) of the vinegar, ¼ cup (3 g) of the dill, 1 tablespoon (15 ml) of the oil and ¼ teaspoon of the salt. Stir well to combine and set aside.

Remove the vegetables from the oven, place on a serving platter, top with dill and serve with the yogurt-dill sauce.

Lemon-Asparagus Baked Rice

Baking rice with aromatics infuses flavor into the rice, and the hands-off bake time allows the cook to do other things while the rice is cooking. Most likely there will be a conversation around the crispy rice on top of the dish—some fight for it, others are happy to pass. I personally prefer a bit of crispy rice on my plate and will fight for it.

Cooking Notes:

- *This recipe works best with medium-sized asparagus. If your asparagus comes bundled with two rubber bands, keep them securely around the asparagus while chopping. The rubber bands help to hold the asparagus together and makes for an easier chopping session.*

Yields 6–8 SERVINGS

2 cups (405 g) long grain rice (I prefer basmati)

1 lb (454 g) medium-sized asparagus, woody ends removed, cut into ½-inch (1.3-cm) pieces

3 tbsp (42 g) unsalted butter

1 cup (160 g) yellow onion, finely diced

2 cloves garlic, chopped

2 tsp (12 g) kosher salt

3½ cups (840 ml) water

2 lemons (zest of 2 lemons, plus more to taste, and 2 tsp [10 ml] of lemon juice)

Heat the oven to 425°F (218°C).

Place the rice and asparagus into a large ceramic baking pan.

In a medium-sized pan, add the butter and melt over medium heat. Add the onion, garlic and salt to the pan. Cook for 5 minutes, stirring occasionally. Add the water, lemon zest and lemon juice to the pan. Increase the heat to high and bring to a boil.

Once the water is boiling, pour the water mixture over the rice. Place into the oven and bake until the edges are crispy and the rice is cooked through, 40 to 45 minutes. If you want the rice to be extra crispy, broil for 1 to 2 minutes. Be sure to keep a watchful eye on the rice so it does not burn.

Remove from the oven and top with additional lemon zest to taste. Serve warm.

Cauliflower Gratin

While some may consider this Cauliflower Gratin a side dish, it is substantial enough to be a main entrée when served with crusty bread and a crisp salad, like the Dijon Butter Lettuce Salad (page 105). I adore this recipe for its ingredients and simple prep. One unexpected addition is egg yolks, which create a custard-like sauce that binds and flavors the gratin, making this baked cauliflower dish rich and filling—and one you will want to enjoy repeatedly.

Cooking Notes:

- *For an easier prep, purchase cauliflower florets. Be sure to mash the cauliflower on a low heat setting on the cooktop. This helps to evaporate any leftover cooking liquid. If you have leftover chicken stock in the fridge, feel free to use it as the cooking liquid.*

Yields 6–8 SERVINGS

2 tbsp (28 g) unsalted butter, plus more for preparing the baking dish

2½ to 3 lb (1.1 to 1.4 kg) cauliflower florets, cut into 1½-inch (3.8-cm) pieces

1½ tsp (9 g) kosher salt

1 tsp (3 g) ground ginger

1 cup (240 ml) cream

1 cup (78 g) panko breadcrumbs

2 egg yolks

2 cups (216 g) Gruyère, grated, divided

1 tsp white wine vinegar

Heat the oven to 425°F (218°C). Butter a shallow gratin dish and set aside.

Fill a large pan with water and bring to a boil over medium-high heat, then add the cauliflower and cook covered until softened and easily pierced with a fork, 10 to 15 minutes. Decrease the heat to low. Strain the cauliflower from the cooking liquid, return the cauliflower to the pan and place back onto the cooktop.

With a potato masher, mash the cauliflower until the desired consistency is achieved. If the cauliflower appears watery, continue to cook until the liquid is reduced. Add the salt, ginger and butter to the cauliflower. Stir to combine. Once the butter is melted, add the cream and panko and continue to stir thoroughly.

Remove from the heat. Stirring constantly, add the egg yolks one at a time until the yolks are well incorporated into the mixture. Add the cheese and vinegar, then stir until melted and well combined.

Pour the mixture into the buttered gratin dish and place into the oven. Bake for 25 minutes. Turn on the broiler to 550°F (288°C) and broil until golden brown, 3 to 5 minutes. Remove from the oven and serve warm.

Roasted Brussels and Carrots with Tahini

Roasted Brussels and Carrots with Tahini is hearty enough to be served as a main dish. The main ingredients are superfoods, high in nutrition and extremely filling. On its own, the tahini sauce is very lemony, but when added to the vegetables, the dish is well balanced. While the vegetables roast, the sauce can be quickly assembled, leaving ample time to tidy the kitchen.

Cooking Notes:

- *Before roasting hearty vegetables, I like to first steam them in the oven, which prepares them for roasting. To steam, place foil over a rimmed baking sheet and seal the edges. Roasting for 40 minutes makes the Brussels sprouts very browned and the leaves crispy. This is how I prefer them. If you prefer them more al dente, decrease the roasting time.*

- *If the carrots have their green tops (which I suggest), remove the leafy ends before roasting, wash thoroughly and use as a final topping.*

Yields 4 MAIN SERVINGS OR 8 SIDE SERVINGS

2 tbsp (30 ml) extra-virgin olive oil, divided

1½ tsp (9 g) kosher salt, divided

1½ lb (680 g) Brussels sprouts, ends removed and halved

1½ lb (680 g) carrots (about 12), peeled and leafy greens removed

½ cup (107 g) tahini paste

3 cloves garlic, chopped

2 lemons, juiced

3 tbsp (45 ml) water

¼ tsp ground cayenne (optional)

For the table: Browned Butter Toast (page 120)

Heat the oven to 500°F (260°C).

Place 1 tablespoon (15 ml) of the oil and ½ teaspoon of the salt into a large mixing bowl. Place the Brussels sprouts into the oil mixture and coat well.

On half of a rimmed sheet pan, place the carrots in a single layer. Distribute 1 tablespoon (15 ml) of the oil and ½ teaspoon of the salt over the carrots. Toss the carrots to evenly coat. Add the Brussels sprouts in a single layer on the other half of the sheet pan and cover the sheet pan tightly with foil.

Cook the Brussels sprouts and carrots for 15 minutes. Remove the foil and reduce the heat to 450°F (232°C). Continue to roast, uncovered, for 25 to 30 minutes, until browned to your liking. Stir the Brussels sprouts and flip the carrots once halfway through the roasting period.

In a small bowl, combine the tahini, garlic, lemon juice, water, cayenne (if using) and ½ teaspoon of the salt. Set aside.

Remove the vegetables from the oven and serve warm drizzled with the tahini sauce and carrot greens.

Spanish Pisto

I love making this dish a day or two before I plan to serve it. The rest time in the refrigerator will allow the flavors to marinate and fully develop. Spanish Pisto can be served in various ways. It is great as a main dish, served alongside soft boiled eggs or with crusty bread and a green salad. It can also be used as a topping for crostini or grilled meats and fishes. This dish has no boundaries, so have fun with it!

Cooking Notes:

· *This recipe is a spin on the classic Spanish dish of the same name.*

· *When roasting the tomatoes, place them stem side down. I have found the tomato holds its shape better when roasting in this position and it is easier to peel the skin when they hold their shape.*

Yields 6–8 SERVINGS

3 medium-sized eggplants, whole

3 red bell peppers, whole

5 large tomatoes, whole

2 tbsp (30 ml) extra-virgin olive oil, divided, plus more for topping

1 cup (160 g) chopped yellow onion

1 tsp sherry vinegar

1¼ tsp (8 g) kosher salt

For the table: Browned Butter Toast (page 120) and Pickled Red Onions (page 124)

Heat the oven to 425°F (218°C). Line a rimmed sheet pan with foil.

Place the eggplants, bell peppers and tomatoes on the sheet pan. Coat the vegetables with 1 tablespoon (15 ml) of the oil and place into the oven. Roast for 1 hour, turning the eggplant every 15 to 20 minutes. Remove from the oven and let cool for 20 minutes.

Place the onion and vinegar into a food processor. Blitz until a paste-like consistency forms.

Remove and discard the stem and seeds from the bell peppers. Remove and discard the tomato skin. Slice open the eggplant and scoop out the flesh and set aside. Add the prepared vegetables and salt to the onion mixture in the food processor.

Pulse and slowly pour in 1 tablespoon (15 ml) of the oil while the vegetables are pureeing. Mix until the vegetables are at the desired consistency.

Pour the mixture into a serving bowl and serve at room temperature or chilled, topped with a drizzle of olive oil.

To add extra flavor, *freshly grate Manchego on top.*

splendid sides

Sides are as critical to the dinner plate as the entrée. Often an afterthought, side dishes deserve the same attention to texture, flavor and technique as entrées. They have the capability to make a meal, and that is an exciting opportunity. What is a well-braised short rib with a decadent sauce if there is no polenta to sop up the goodness?

This chapter is dedicated to developing sides that not only complement the entrée, but can also stand on their own. These recipes are simple to make and clever in ingredients and technique. Take note—simple and clever does not always mean quick. Some recipes will take time to develop flavor, like the Pineapple Coeur à la Crème with Apples (page 109), and others will not, like the Lemony Caesar Salad (page 98) or Herbes de Provence Couscous with Buttermilk (page 97).

Fancy titles aside, these recipes are approachable. Most of them require beginner-level skills, but vary in the number of steps needed and techniques used. With each meal, the goal is to orchestrate harmony and balance on the plate. While an entrée anchors the dinner plate, it is the sides that will ultimately complete the meal.

Duck Fat–Roasted Cauliflower

The unique flavor of duck fat complements the unmatched essence of roasted cauliflower in this savory and simple recipe. Whether this dish is saved for special occasions, or if it becomes a weekly tradition, it is one to be cherished.

Cooking Notes:

- *Duck fat can be found at high-end grocers, specialty food stores or online. It is one of my favorite ingredients to keep handy to create elegant and delicious dishes.*

- *To make prep time easier, purchase precut cauliflower florets. For easy cleanup, line the sheet pan with foil.*

- *If you tend to eat the cauliflower quickly and wish there were more, increase the amount of cauliflower used to 10 cups (1.1 kg) and add a smidge more duck fat and salt. If you do not feel like chopping garlic, you can omit it.*

Yields 4–5 SERVINGS

1½ tbsp (18 g) duck fat

1 tsp kosher salt

8 cups (860 g) cauliflower florets

10 sprigs fresh thyme

10 leaves fresh sage

4 cloves garlic, crushed

For the table: Herbed Crème Fraiche (page 123) and Pickled Red Onions (page 124)

Heat the oven to 450°F (232°C). Line a rimmed sheet pan with foil.

Place the duck fat into a large bowl. If it is solidified, allow the duck fat to rest for about 10 minutes, or gently warm to help it begin to liquefy. Add the salt and stir to combine. Place the cauliflower florets into the bowl and toss to coat.

Using a slotted spoon, evenly place the cauliflower in a single layer onto the sheet pan. Top with the thyme and sage. Place into the oven and roast for 45 minutes. Stir once after 20 minutes. When there are 5 minutes left in the roasting process, add the garlic to the cauliflower and continue to cook.

Remove from the oven and serve warm.

Herbes de Provence Couscous with Buttermilk

A quick-cooking couscous seasoned with herbes de Provence is a dream come true. Ready in under 10 minutes, this side dish is a charming partner to several main dishes. Don't let the buttermilk hold you back from making this recipe. Buttermilk adds a salty and tangy flavor—similar to plain yogurt—that uniquely complements the fragrant couscous.

Cooking Notes:

- *The floral note of this couscous pairs well with several dishes; however, it can clash with others. Choose to pair with mildly seasoned meats and vegetables.*

- *This recipe can easily be doubled, but do not double the herbes de Provence or the salt. Increase these ingredients by a pinch or two and then season to taste. Be sure to read the instructions on the couscous and adjust accordingly. The 1:1 ratio applied to this recipe is for a particular brand of couscous—the one you use may be different. Plain yogurt can be substituted for the buttermilk.*

Yields 4–5 SERVINGS

1½ cups (360 ml) low-sodium chicken stock

½ tsp herbes de Provence

½ tsp kosher salt

1 tbsp (15 ml) extra-virgin olive oil

1½ cups (268 g) couscous

1 tsp red wine vinegar

Buttermilk, to taste (optional)

For the table: Pickled Red Onions (page 124)

In a saucepan, add the stock, herbes de Provence, salt and oil. Bring to a boil. Add the couscous to the cooking liquid and stir. Remove from the heat, cover and let sit for 4 to 5 minutes.

Remove the lid and fluff with a fork. Stir in the vinegar.

Serve the couscous warm and with a side of buttermilk, if desired.

Lemony Caesar Salad

While this salad may appear basic, it is anything but ordinary. It is a bright and lovely salad made delicious by the homemade dressing. I cannot stress enough how important it is to choose a good quality olive oil. Quality oil begets an excellent dressing that begets a superior salad.

Cooking Notes:

- Do not let the anchovy paste scare you away from this recipe. Anchovy paste—when used sparingly—brings a depth of flavor that is necessary in a Caesar salad.
- Due to my great love of Parmesan, I err on the side of extra cheese in this salad. However, the more Parmesan added, the saltier it becomes. Adjust to your preference and also consider what you are serving alongside the salad.

Yields 6–8 SERVINGS

2 tbsp (30 ml) good quality extra-virgin olive oil

2 lemons (2 tbsp [30 ml] juice, zest of 1 lemon)

2 tbsp (30 ml) water

¼ tsp black pepper

¼ tsp white wine vinegar

1½ tsp (12 g) anchovy paste

3 heads romaine lettuce (about 1½ lb [680g]), chopped

¾ cup (93 g) finely grated Parmesan

For the table: Pickled Red Onions (page 124)

Add the oil, lemon juice, zest, water, pepper, vinegar and anchovy paste to a large bowl. Whisk until combined.

Place the romaine into the bowl and toss to coat. Chill in the fridge and top with the Parmesan before serving.

To add extra flavor, add cherry tomatoes.

Baked Gorgonzola Polenta

Polenta is traditionally made on the cooktop and served on a wooden cutting board. It is quite the culinary experience. While this version is not classic, it is still a versatile dish that can be served with most any hearty sauce, roasted vegetable or meat.

Cooking Notes:

- *It is critical to slowly add the cornmeal in small portions to the chicken stock. A quick pour of all the cornmeal into the cooking liquid will not end well—I speak from experience. Be sure to follow the instruction to stir the polenta every 15 minutes. Set a kitchen timer to remind you.*

- *Gorgonzola is a strong—and some may call a "stinky"—cheese, which I appreciate. Although the Gorgonzola is subtle in this recipe, its presence is undeniable. Pair with a dish that will complement this characteristic, like the Porcini Beef Ragù (page 69) or roasted vegetables. This polenta is intentionally less salty to allow for pairings with more robust and salty dishes.*

Yields 4–6 SERVINGS

2 tbsp (30 ml) extra-virgin olive oil

¾ cup (120 g) diced yellow onion

4 cups (960 ml) low-sodium chicken stock

1 cup (122 g) coarse cornmeal

2 tbsp (28 g) unsalted butter

¼ tsp kosher salt, plus more to finish

1 cup (144 g) crumbled Gorgonzola

For the table: Coconut Mushroom Gravy (page 131) and Smothered Tomatoes (page 127)

Heat the oven to 350°F (177°C).

In a large oven-safe saucepan set over medium heat, add the oil and onion and cook until soft, 5 to 6 minutes.

Add the chicken stock, increase the heat to high and bring to a boil. Whisk continuously and slowly add the cornmeal, about 2 tablespoons (15 g) at a time. Cover the polenta and place into the oven.

Cook for 45 minutes—stirring every 15 minutes to prevent burning and clumping—or until the cornmeal is cooked all the way, soft in appearance and the liquid is absorbed.

Remove the polenta from the oven. Add the butter and the salt. Stir well. Once the butter is melted, add the Gorgonzola. Stir until the Gorgonzola is melted and distributed throughout. Salt to taste and serve immediately.

Mashed Peas with Bacon Breadcrumbs

Peas are underappreciated and should make an appearance in your kitchen. They are quick to cook and offer an array of benefits, from their nutrition to flavor to versatility. Some days I simply toss peas in butter and serve as-is. Mashed Peas with Bacon Breadcrumbs is a comforting dish that is sweet, salty and crunchy. The crème fraiche and bacon fat breadcrumbs tie this side dish together. What a delicious way to bring peas to your table!

Cooking Notes:

- *You can use either fresh or frozen peas in this recipe. Fresh peas will take a bit longer to cook than frozen. To check for doneness, simply remove a pea from the boiling water, let it cool and taste. The pea should be soft to the bite (avoid al dente).*

- *If you do not have an immersion blender, use a regular blender.*

Yields 5–6 SERVINGS

6 oz (170 g) bacon (about 6 slices)

1 cup (80 g) panko breadcrumbs

1 lb (454 g) peas

2 tbsp (28 g) unsalted butter

4 oz (113 g) crème fraiche

½ tsp kosher salt

8 to 10 fresh mint leaves, chopped, plus more for topping

2 tsp (10 ml) fresh lemon juice

For the table: Browned Butter Toast (page 120) and Pickled Red Onions (page 124)

In a skillet set over medium heat, cook the bacon until crispy, 11 to 14 minutes. Do not discard the rendered fat. Remove the bacon to a paper towel-lined plate. Allow to cool for about 5 minutes. Once cool, crumble the bacon and set aside.

Remove half of the bacon fat from the skillet, leaving about 2 tablespoons (30 ml). Add the breadcrumbs and cook on medium-low heat until golden, about 5 minutes. Remove the breadcrumbs from the skillet and place onto a paper towel-lined plate.

Fill a medium pan with water and bring to a boil. Add the peas and cook until softened, 5 to 6 minutes. Strain the peas and place back into the pan. Add the butter and stir until it is melted and has coated the peas. Add the crème fraiche and salt. Stir to combine.

Use an immersion blender to puree the pea mixture until smooth. Stir in the mint and lemon juice.

Place the mashed peas into a serving bowl and top with the bacon, breadcrumbs and fresh mint.

Dijon Butter Lettuce Salad

This Dijon Butter Lettuce Salad is delicious, wholesome and simple enough in preparation to become a go-to recipe. I serve it to my family almost weekly and at most gatherings—per the request of my friends. It is a salad that is dear to me.

Cooking Notes:

- *My favorite part of this salad is the vinaigrette. I recommend using a Dijon that you like, as it is prominent in the dressing. Double the recipe to ensure you have extra dressing on hand for other uses. Since the vinaigrette is stored in the fridge, the olive oil will solidify. Allow it to come to room temperature before use. If you need to liquefy it quickly, add a splash or two of olive oil and balsamic and stir.*

- *Sliced cherry tomatoes and crumbled goat cheese are nice additions to the salad.*

- *The ingredients can easily be halved if you want a smaller portion. I often use a 7-ounce (198-g) bag of chopped butter lettuce.*

Yields 4–8 SERVINGS

¼ cup (60 ml) Dijon mustard

½ tsp granulated garlic

½ tsp kosher salt

2 tbsp (30 ml) balsamic vinegar

½ cup (120 ml) extra-virgin olive oil

2 hothouse cucumbers (about 1½ lb [680 g]), peeled

14 oz (396 g) chopped butter lettuce

Fresh cilantro (optional), chopped

For the table: Pickled Red Onions (page 124)

Place the Dijon, garlic, salt, vinegar and oil into a canning jar and seal tightly. Shake until the ingredients are incorporated. If the Dijon sticks to the sides of the jar, use a whisk to incorporate.

With a vegetable peeler, slice the cucumber into thin strips. Cut the strips into bite-sized pieces. Place the cucumber pieces, lettuce and cilantro, if using, into a salad bowl. Pour the desired amount of Dijon vinaigrette over the salad. Toss and serve immediately. Any remaining vinaigrette should be stored in an airtight container in the fridge.

Braised Green Beans

There are benefits to revisiting classic, simple recipes. These types of recipes are reminders that memorable meals do not have to be time consuming or require a lot of ingredients. While Braised Green Beans may seem unassuming, it is a recipe that is nourishing and familiar—like an old friend. This recipe yields a large batch of tender green beans ready to be eaten the day of or throughout the week.

Cooking Notes:

- *Do not fear the large amount of salt; it will be combined with the water to make a brine. If saltier green beans are preferred, add an additional teaspoon of kosher salt to increase the measurement to 2 tablespoons (36 g). If you opt to add bacon, decrease the amount of salt.*

- *To prevent stringy beans, you can either snap and string the green beans before braising, or look for prepackaged beans. If you don't have the time, don't worry—the recipe will still work.*

- *Second-day green beans, when given time to develop even more umami in their salty brine, are a treat. Try serving the beans cold with Herbed Crème Fraiche (page 123).*

- *This recipe intentionally makes a large batch. It can easily be halved.*

Yields 8 SERVINGS

24 oz (680 g) fresh green beans

8 cups (1.9 L) water

1 tbsp plus 2 tsp (30 g) kosher salt

For the Table: Coconut Mushroom Gravy (page 131) and Herbed Crème Fraiche (page 123)

Place the green beans and water into a large pan. Bring to a boil over high heat, about 10 minutes. Once boiling, add the salt and stir.

Reduce the heat to low and cover the pan with the lid slightly tilted. Simmer for 15 minutes, or until the green beans reach your desired doneness.

To add extra flavor, *add 2 to 3 strips of bacon to the pan before boiling the water.*

Pineapple Coeur à la Crème with Apples

There is something about pineapples and their old-world status as a delicacy that makes me regard this recipe with nostalgia. Pineapple Coeur à la Crème with Apples is a "fancy" recipe that is incredibly simple to make. With under 10 minutes of prep time and a 24-hour set time in the fridge, it is an easy recipe that can be whipped up for the following day's meal. Serve at breakfast, lunch or dinner, and this spreadable cheese will be the star of mealtime. For a sweet and savory option, top crostini with prosciutto and this coeur à la crème.

Cooking Notes:

- *To soften the cream cheese, leave it at room temperature for 3 to 5 hours. It is important the cream cheese is softened prior to whipping to help achieve the right consistency. Do not skip this step.*

- *Be sure to purchase chopped canned pineapple. Cheesecloth is necessary for this recipe to be successful.*

- *Allow for the full 24-hour rest in the fridge. When flipping the cheese out of the strainer onto a serving plate, make sure the cheese is centered on the plate to prevent any of the mixture from landing on the side of the plate or the floor.*

Yields 6–8 SERVINGS

1 (8-oz [227-g]) can chopped pineapple

8 oz (227 g) cream cheese, softened

¾ cup (180 ml) heavy whipping cream

2 tbsp (30 ml) honey

Pinch of kosher salt

1 tsp sugar

¼ tsp vanilla extract

Apple slices, to serve

Reserve 1 teaspoon of juice from the canned pineapple. Drain the remaining juice and rough chop the pineapple.

Place the cream cheese into a large mixing bowl and using a mixer with a paddle attachment, beat the cream cheese at medium speed for 2 minutes.

Replace the paddle attachment with the whisking attachment. While whipping at a medium-high speed, add the cream in a steady stream. Add the honey, salt, sugar, vanilla extract and pineapple juice. Whip for 1 minute. Turn off the mixer and gently fold in the chopped pineapple.

Line a mesh strainer with cheesecloth. Suspend the strainer over a medium-sized bowl. Make sure there is space between the bottom of the strainer and the bowl to allow the excess liquid to drain. Pour the mixture into the strainer and fold the cheesecloth over the top. Place in the fridge for 24 hours.

Before serving, place a small serving plate on top of the mesh strainer. While holding the plate and strainer, flip over so the coeur à la crème falls out of the strainer onto the serving plate. Serve immediately with apple slices.

Cucumber Olive Saffron Salad

The base of cucumbers, Kalamata olives and saffron makes a delicious salad that is both refreshing and filling. The hassle-free components of this recipe are easy to keep on hand throughout the year. It is quick to assemble and easy to love.

Cooking Notes:

- *Salting and drying the cucumbers one hour before assembling the salad will help them to maintain their crunch.*

- *Crumbled goat cheese is a nice addition to the salad; ¼ cup (38 g) is the perfect amount.*

- *This salad will keep in the fridge for up to 2 days, but it will get soggy the longer it sits.*

Yields 4–6 SERVINGS

1 lb (454 g) Persian cucumbers, sliced

¼ tsp kosher salt, plus more for finishing

2 tsp (10 ml) red wine vinegar

2 tbsp (30 ml) extra-virgin olive oil

Pinch of saffron threads

¾ cup (104 g) Kalamata olives, halved

¼ cup (3 g) fresh mint leaves, torn

¼ cup (3 g) fresh dill, chopped

In a medium-sized bowl, add the cucumbers and salt. Stir to combine. Put in the fridge for one hour.

Meanwhile, combine the vinegar, oil and saffron in a small bowl. Whisk and set aside for at least 30 minutes.

Remove the cucumbers from the bowl in the fridge and place onto a towel-lined cutting board. Pat the cucumbers dry. Rinse and dry the bowl. Place the cucumbers back into the dried bowl and add the olives, mint, dill and the saffron oil. Toss to coat well. Salt to taste.

Serve immediately or place back into the fridge to chill.

Smothered Marsala Shallots

One of the many appeals of this recipe is the minimal effort it takes to create an elegant and flavorful side that will look gorgeous on your table for a dinner party, brunch or a special family dinner. The shallots are versatile and pair well with several dishes, from salads and sandwiches to scrambled eggs and steak.

Cooking Notes:

- *There will be enough shallots to cover three wheels of Brie. I suggest serving one wheel of cheese and reserving the shallots for the next day.*

- *The smothered shallots can be pureed into a jam-like consistency using a food processor or blender. If the shallots are pureed, add a bit of water until the desired thickness is achieved. They will continue to develop flavor as they sit in the fridge. Like many recipes, it is even more delicious on day two.*

- *The shallots will need to be cut into thirds. This can be done either horizontally to create more bite-sized pieces or vertically to create a more curated look.*

Yields APPROXIMATELY 4 TO 6 CUPS (782 TO 1173 G)

1½ lb (680 g) shallots, peeled and cut into thirds

2 sprigs fresh basil, chopped, plus additional for topping

½ cup (120 ml) extra-virgin olive oil

½ cup (120 ml) dry Marsala

1 tbsp (16 g) sugar

1 tsp kosher salt

¼ tsp black pepper

2 tsp (10 ml) white wine vinegar

Brie wheel (optional)

For the table: Browned Butter Toast (page 120)

Place the shallots and the basil sprigs into a medium-sized skillet. Pour the oil and Marsala over the shallots. Stir to coat. Add the sugar, salt and pepper. Stir to combine. Cover and cook over medium-low heat for 15 to 20 minutes.

Remove the lid and stir the shallots. Increase the heat to medium and scrape up any bits that have stuck to the bottom of the pan and continue to cook for 15 minutes. Stir occasionally.

Add the vinegar and stir. Remove from the heat and cool for 10 minutes. Remove the basil sprigs. If using the Brie, remove the outer layer from the cheese and place the Brie on a rimmed serving platter. Pour the shallots over the Brie, top with chopped basil and serve with crusty bread. If you prefer to skip the Brie, top the shallots with the basil and serve as-is.

Rosemary Garlic Sour Cream Mashed Potatoes

This recipe is about technique. Instead of adding cold butter, milk and seasoning after the potatoes have boiled—as many recipes instruct—this recipe infuses flavor from the beginning of the cooking process and adds warmed ingredients to the cooked potatoes. The result is incredibly creamy and flavorful mashed potatoes.

Cooking Notes:

- *Don't skip the step to melt the butter. When the warm, melted butter and half-and-half mixture is added to the hot mashed potatoes, it continues to keep the potatoes warm, and the flavors of rosemary and garlic are infused in the potatoes.*

- *Do be sure to remove all of the aromatics before mashing. Smaller potato pieces will take less time to cook.*

- *For a less tangy flavor, substitute crème fraiche for the sour cream. Consider adding a bit of lemon zest to finish.*

Yields 10–12 SERVINGS

12 tbsp (168 g) unsalted butter

¼ cup (60 ml) half-and-half, cream or whole milk

6 cloves garlic, crushed

4 sprigs rosemary, divided

4 lb (1.8 kg) Yukon gold potatoes, peeled and cut into pieces

2 tsp (12 g) kosher salt, plus more for finishing

1 cup (250 g) sour cream, room temperature

For the table: Coconut Mushroom Gravy (page 131)

Place the butter, half-and-half, garlic and 3 rosemary sprigs into a small saucepan. Melt the butter mixture over low heat. Keep warm.

Bring a large pot of water with 1 rosemary sprig to a boil, add the potatoes and cook until easily pierced with a fork, 25 to 30 minutes. Strain the potatoes and remove the rosemary. Reduce the heat to low.

Return the potatoes to the pot and place back onto the burner. Mash with a potato masher. Add the salt and continue to mash, stirring occasionally.

Remove the garlic and rosemary from the butter mixture.

Once the potatoes are well mashed and smooth, add the melted butter mixture. Stir to combine and turn off the heat.

Add the sour cream to the potatoes and continue to mash and stir until the desired consistency is achieved. Salt to taste and cover to keep warm until serving.

Arugula and Grape Cilantro Salad

All the components of this salad work beautifully together. The spice from the arugula and the acid from the lemon are balanced by the sweetness of the honey and grapes. The cilantro and seasoned rice wine vinegar bring a brightness to the overall dish. Arugula and Grape Cilantro Salad is a wonderful table partner for grilled or roasted meats.

Cooking Notes:

- *If the grapes are tossed with the salad, they tend to fall to the bottom of the bowl. I recommend adding them to the top of each individual salad, or if serving in a larger bowl, add after the salad has been tossed. If the grapes are small, you don't need to halve them.*

- *It is important to use seasoned rice wine vinegar, not rice wine vinegar. Seasoned rice wine vinegar has sugar and salt in it, which adds a depth of flavor to the vinaigrette.*

Yields 4–6 SERVINGS

1 tbsp (15 ml) extra-virgin olive oil

3 tbsp (45 ml) seasoned rice wine vinegar

1 lemon (zest and juice)

1 tbsp (15 ml) honey

¼ tsp kosher salt

5 oz (142 g) arugula

1 cup (15 g) fresh cilantro, lightly packed

1½ cups (210 g) purple grapes, halved

For the table: Pickled Red Onions (page 124)

In a small bowl, combine the oil, vinegar, lemon zest and juice, honey and salt. Whisk until thoroughly combined. Set aside.

When ready to serve, place the arugula and cilantro into a large serving bowl. Pour the desired amount of vinaigrette over the salad and toss. Top with the grapes. Serve immediately.

for the table

For the Table recipes encompass simple food at its best—little partners for sides and entrees that help to elevate meals. These additions for the table are not meant to be fussy. Containing only a handful of ingredients each, these recipes are meant to be thrown together easily. They become the crunchy, salty and sour accessories to the side and entrée. By providing these additional elements throughout the meal, you've silently encouraged diners to personalize their plate.

Many of these recipes can be made in advance and stored in the fridge to be used throughout the week. There is no need to buy special ingredients; use what is readily available to complete the recipe. Don't have crème fraiche for Herbed Crème Fraiche (page 123)? Try sour cream and loosen with a touch of whipping cream or water. Grabbed beefsteak tomatoes at the market instead of cherry? That's okay; cut the tomatoes into small pieces and use instead for Smothered Tomatoes (page 127). Is there a mound of yellow onions needing to be used? Substitute these for the red variety in Pickled Red Onions (page 124). Only sandwich bread in the pantry? Use these slices for Browned Butter Toast (page 120).

Be creative and confident; utilize your pantry and cravings to create your own flavors. It is your table; make it personal.

Browned Butter Toast

Yields 4–6 SERVINGS

1 French baguette

3 to 6 tbsp (42 to 84 g) salted butter

Pinch of kosher salt

While this recipe may seem simple in its ingredients, the result of gently frying bread in browned butter creates a magical little side. It is more than the sum of its parts. A plate piled high with Browned Butter Toast is a perfect companion to any meal. As my best friend says, "Hot crusty bread and butter gets a kid through any vegetable." I believe this is true for adults as well.

Cooking Notes:

- *To keep the toasted bread warm while toasting the remaining slices, place on a cooling rack in a warm oven.*

- *If you do not have a cast-iron skillet, you can use a heavy flat-bottom skillet.*

- *Try to use good quality bread and butter. The amount of butter used will depend on the size of the baguette—a small baguette typically needs 3 tablespoons (42 g), while a larger baguette will need up to 6 tablespoons (84 g). Remember to add more butter if necessary.*

Cut the baguette into quarters to make four smaller loaves. Halve the loaves by slicing through middle of the bread, hot dog style. There should be a total of eight rectangular bread slices. If these seem too big, halve one more time.

In a large cast-iron skillet, add 3 tablespoons (42 g) of the butter. Over medium heat, melt the butter until it starts to brown, 5 to 6 minutes. Add a pinch of salt to the butter. Swirl the pan to coat the pan with the butter.

Place the bread cut-side down in the skillet. Cook for 2½ minutes. Flip the bread and continue to cook for 1 to 2 minutes. Thinner pieces will need less time to toast. Remove the slices as they finish browning.

If making an additional batch, remove the skillet from the heat and wipe with a paper towel. Repeat the cooking steps until all bread is toasted. Serve warm.

To add extra flavor, *a generous smear of whole grain mustard would be delicious. As would a bit of Brie.*

Herbed Crème Fraiche

Herbed Crème Fraiche is a simple recipe that can add an earthy creaminess to vegetables, bread, pasta and meats.

Cooking Notes:

- *The crème fraiche will keep in the fridge for a week. Any longer and the herbs begin to lose some of their freshness.*

- *Play around with the herbs to create flavor combinations that reflect your palate and the seasons.*

- *Herbed Crème Fraiche intentionally has no salt added because it is intended to accompany dishes that have been properly salted.*

- *This recipe is easily doubled.*

Yields 8 SERVINGS

8 oz (227 g) crème fraiche

⅓ cup (6 g) fresh basil, lightly packed, chopped

⅓ cup (6 g) fresh tarragon, lightly packed, chopped

Zest of 1 lemon

In a small bowl, combine the crème fraiche, basil, tarragon and lemon zest. Stir and place in the fridge to chill, at least 15 minutes. Serve cold.

Pickled Red Onions

These onions are versatile and incredibly delicious. The preparation is very simple: slice, boil and pour. Whether used for salads, sandwiches, pastas, tacos or grilled meats, pickled red onions are one of a good cook's best kept secrets.

Cooking Notes:

- *The pith does not have to be completely removed from the lemon peel. Try to get as much as your patience allows.*

- *You can omit the lemon if you don't want citrus notes. If the brine is too tangy for your liking, add a bit of water to mellow the flavor.*

Yields APPROXIMATELY
3 CUPS (627 G)

1 lemon

1 large red onion, halved and thinly sliced

1 cup (240 ml) seasoned rice wine vinegar

1 tsp mustard seed

¼ tsp kosher salt

½ tsp sugar

½ tsp honey

Pinch of red pepper flakes

Cut off one end of the lemon. Stabilize the lemon on the flat end and use a vegetable peeler to slowly peel one strip of the lemon, starting from the top and moving down to the bottom. The peel should be about 3 inches (8 cm) long. With a paring knife, carefully scrape off as much white pith as possible. Set aside.

Place the onion into a large, heat-proof bowl and set aside.

Place the vinegar, mustard seeds, salt, sugar, honey, red pepper flakes and lemon peel into a small saucepan. Bring to a boil over high heat. Pour the brine over the onion.

Press down on the onion (I use the back of a large spatula) to completely submerge. Cool for 30 minutes and place into the fridge. Strain before serving.

Smothered Tomatoes

I cannot praise this recipe enough. Whether it is used as a dip for breads, a topper for grilled meats and fish, a sauce for pasta or an accoutrement for hummus, its versatility makes it a constant companion at my table. Be creative with how you use it.

Cooking Notes:

- *This recipe can easily be doubled.*
- *Smothered Tomatoes, like many recipes, develops more flavor over a 24-hour period of refrigeration.*
- *The tomatoes can be gently reheated on the cooktop.*

Yields 4 SERVINGS

4 cups (638 g) cherry tomatoes, halved

¼ cup (60 ml) balsamic vinegar

¾ cups (180 ml) extra-virgin olive oil

2 sprigs rosemary

2 to 3 cloves garlic, chopped

¾ tsp kosher salt

Crusty bread

Place the tomatoes, vinegar, oil, rosemary, garlic and salt into a sauté pan. Cook over medium heat and bring to a simmer. Reduce the heat to medium-low and continue to cook for 20 minutes or until the tomatoes are softened and the cooking liquid is reduced.

Serve warm with crusty bread.

To add extra flavor, *add a pinch of red pepper flakes for a bit of heat.*

Garlic Coeur à la Crème

I have found that cheese can elevate a dining experience simply by being on the table. Garlic Coeur à la Crème is a bright and flavorful spin on a classic French dessert, and is the perfect accoutrement for any meal. It is incredibly versatile—it can be served with items like sandwiches, fresh vegetables or pasta—and requires little prep.

Cooking Notes:

- *You will need cheesecloth for this recipe. The cheesecloth will help absorb excess moisture from the mixture, creating a concentrated ball of creamy garlic cheese. This recipe needs 24 hours of straining in the cheesecloth to produce the best result. Plan accordingly.*

- *Adjust the salt content depending on what dipping "vessels" you intend to serve with this dip. For fresh, raw vegetables and crusty bread, keep the salt as-is. If using salty chips and crackers, err on the side of caution and reduce the salt by half. You can always add more salt, but can never take any away.*

Yields 6–8 SERVINGS

8 oz (227 g) cream cheese, softened at room temperature for 3 to 5 hours

¾ cup (180 ml) heavy whipping cream

1 tsp white wine vinegar

½ tsp kosher salt

5 cloves garlic, chopped

Place the cream cheese into a large mixing bowl. Using a stand mixer (or a hand-held mixer) with a paddle attachment, beat the cream cheese at medium speed for 2 minutes.

Replace the paddle attachment with the whisking attachment. While whipping at a medium-high speed, add the cream in a steady stream. Add the vinegar and salt. Whip for 1 minute. Turn off the mixer and gently stir in the garlic.

Line a mesh strainer with cheesecloth. Pour the mixture into the cheesecloth-lined strainer. Suspend the strainer over a medium-sized bowl (make sure there is space between the bottom of the strainer and the bowl to ensure the removal of excess liquid). Fold the cheesecloth over the top of the mixture. Place in the fridge for 24 hours.

Before serving, unfold the top of the cheesecloth and place a small serving plate on top of the mesh strainer. While holding the plate and strainer, flip over, allowing the coeur à la crème to fall out of the strainer onto the serving plate. Serve immediately with crackers or toasted bread.

To add extra flavor, *top with freshly chopped basil, mint, tarragon or cilantro.*

Coconut Mushroom Gravy

Creamy, rich and full of umami, this Coconut Mushroom Gravy will be a table standout no matter what it is served alongside. This gravy has appeared on my table to complement green beans, steak, pasta and Baked Gorgonzola Polenta (page 101). It is even hearty enough to be served on toast as a meal. Be creative with how you choose to use it.

Cooking Notes:

- *Choose whatever variety of mushrooms you prefer. I like to use shiitake and oyster mushrooms, but these types of wild mushrooms can be a bit pricey and require additional work to remove the stems. Portabella or white mushrooms will also work just fine.*

- *This recipe can easily be doubled. As with any recipe that is doubled, be sure to monitor the salt content; start with the original measurement of salt and add more to taste at the end of the cooking process.*

Yields 6 SERVINGS

3 tbsp (45 ml) extra-virgin olive oil, divided

3 cloves garlic, chopped

1 lb (454 g) mushrooms, chopped, divided

¾ tsp kosher salt, divided, plus more to taste

2 sprigs basil

1 (13.5-oz [400-ml]) can coconut milk

1 tsp ground ginger

In a medium-sized skillet set over low heat, warm 2 tablespoons (30 ml) of the olive oil with the garlic. Cook for 4 minutes, stirring occasionally.

Increase the heat to medium. Add half of the mushrooms and ¼ teaspoon of the salt to the skillet. Cook for 5 minutes, stirring occasionally. Push the mushrooms to the outside of the pan. Add 1 tablespoon (15 ml) of the oil. Once it has heated, about 20 seconds, add the second half of the mushrooms, basil and ¼ teaspoon of the salt to the center of the pan. Stir to combine and cook until the mushrooms are softened, about 5 minutes. Stir occasionally.

Reduce the heat to low. Add the coconut milk, ¼ teaspoon of the salt and the ginger to the mushrooms. Stir to combine. Bring to a simmer for 10 to 15 minutes. Salt to taste and serve warm.

divine desserts

Sugary bites need not be bound to mealtime. A mid-day scoop of Wedding Cake Ice Cream (page 138) or a morning nibble on a Brown Sugar–Orange Sables (page 137) is liberating. I encourage consuming these little luxuries at any time of the day. The treats in this chapter should be enjoyed before, after and in-between meals.

Many of these recipes use a hands-off approach to prepare and require little cook time. Delicate yet forward in their foundational flavor, they are not overwhelmingly sweet, because the use of too much sugar can be off-putting. Sweetness should not be domineering, but complementary.

These treats combine playful flavors and delicate sweetness to offer enticing morsels—enjoy at your leisure.

Cilantro-Mint Ice

Cilantro-Mint Ice is a unique and refreshing dessert. Many consider cilantro to be a savory ingredient, but when paired with mint and simple syrup, it can be delicious in sweet treats. The use of fresh herbs and citrus makes this a fragrant and bold frozen treat. Enjoy on a hot summer day with friends.

Cooking Notes:

- *Be sure to peel the lemons before juicing.*

- *If you prefer your ices to be extra sweet, add ¾ cup (180 ml) of the simple syrup instead of the ½ cup (120 ml).*

- *A splash or two of rum is a nice addition.*

Yields 4–6 SERVINGS

2 lemons, plus more for topping

1 cup (200 g) sugar

4 cups (960 ml) water, divided

2 cups (30 g) fresh cilantro leaves, thick stalks removed

2 cups (60 g) fresh mint leaves, plus more for serving

Pinch of kosher salt

Peel four 4-inch (10.2-cm) strips from the lemons. Juice the lemons, resulting in 2 tablespoons (30 ml) juice. To make the simple syrup, in a saucepan, combine the sugar, 2 of the lemon strips and 1 cup (240 ml) of the water. Cook over low heat until the sugar is dissolved, about 15 minutes. Stir occasionally. Remove the simple syrup from the heat and let cool for 15 minutes. Remove the 2 lemon peels and discard.

Add the lemon juice, 3 cups (720 ml) of the water, the cilantro, mint, ½ cup (120 ml) of the simple syrup and salt into a blender. Blend. Strain into a large, sealable container. Place the 2 additional lemon peels into the container. Seal and place into the freezer. Every hour, for 2 hours, shake the container to break up the forming ice. After 2 hours, shake every 30 minutes until a slush-like consistency develops.

Serve frozen with lemon wedges and mint.

To add extra flavor, *add a few pieces of fresh peeled ginger to the simple syrup, just remember to remove the ginger after cooking and before pureeing.*

Brown Sugar–Orange Sables

I adore sables. They are bite-sized, buttery and not too sugary. Part of the joy of making these is the shelf life of the dough. It can be frozen for up to 1 month and thawed in the refrigerator when ready to use. I like to keep a few bundles readily available just in case I get a craving. I particularly enjoy Brown Sugar–Orange Sables with a morning cappuccino.

Cooking Notes:

- *The dough will be slightly sticky. Don't worry, this is okay.*

- *These sables have a more robust, rich flavor due to the use of brown sugar instead of white sugar.*

- *Keep in mind that the number of cookies baked depends upon how large the dough cylinders are and how thick the dough is cut.*

Yields ABOUT 40 COOKIES

1 cup (210 g) brown sugar

2 cups (321 g) flour

¼ tsp kosher salt

2 tsp (8 g) baking powder

2 sticks (½ lb [227 g]) unsalted butter, cold and cut into cubes

3 oranges (zest of 3 oranges and 2 tablespoons [30 ml] fresh orange juice)

4 egg yolks

In a food processor, combine the sugar, flour, salt and baking powder. Blitz four or five times until combined.

Add the butter to the flour mixture and blitz until crumbly. Add the zest, juice and egg yolks to the food processor and process until combined.

Divide the dough into two balls. Place one dough ball onto a sheet of plastic wrap or parchment. Shape the dough into a cylinder, 1½ inches (3.8 cm) thick. Repeat this step with the second dough ball. Wrap the cylinders in plastic wrap and refrigerate for 3 hours, or up to 24 hours.

When ready to bake, heat the oven to 325°F (163°C).

Slice the cookies into ½-inch (1.3-cm)-thick rounds. Place onto a silicone baking mat or a parchment-lined sheet pan and bake for 12 to 13 minutes. Only cook one sheet pan of cookies at a time and do not overbake. These cookies will look underdone, but that is how they are supposed to be. Remove from the oven and place the sheet pan onto a cooling rack. Let the cookies cool completely, about 15 minutes.

To add extra flavor, *a pinch of cinnamon or ground cardamom can be added to the flour mixture.*

Wedding Cake Ice Cream

Homemade ice cream is rewarding to make and serve. This recipe is approachable with its minimal steps and ingredients. Wedding Cake Ice Cream can stand alone or be served alongside other desserts. Serve a scoop or two topped with crumbled Brown Sugar–Orange Sables (page 137), toasted chopped pecans or fresh berries.

Cooking Notes:

- *It is imperative to temper the egg yolk mixture with the hot half-and-half. Do not let this mixture cool or come to room temperature. Tempering the yolks with the hot liquid is the cooking process for the yolks. The tempered yolks make this ice cream base a custard, which yields a rich and thick ice cream.*

Yields 4–8 SERVINGS

3 cups (720 ml) half-and-half

¼ tsp almond extract

2 tsp (10 ml) vanilla extract

5 large egg yolks

¾ cup (160 g) sugar

Pour the half-and-half, almond extract and vanilla extract into a small saucepan. Cook over medium-low heat on the cooktop for 15 minutes.

While the half-and-half mixture warms, place the egg yolks and sugar into a large mixing bowl. Whisk until combined.

Once the half-and-half has been warmed for 15 minutes, work quickly to temper the yolk mixture with the half-and-half mixture. To temper the yolks, whisk the eggs quickly while slowly adding the warm liquid—about ¼ cup (60 ml) at a time—until all the liquid is combined.

Cover the bowl and place into the fridge. Let it chill for at least 6 hours and up to 24 hours.

Place the ice cream mixture into an ice cream maker and mix for 20 minutes, or until the ice cream is thickened to the desired consistency.

Serve immediately for soft serve, or place in a freezer-safe container and freeze for a firmer texture, a minimum of 4 hours.

Tiramisu Dip

Tiramisu Dip is a simple variation of the classic—albeit labor intensive—tiramisu. This recipe is a "stir-to-combine-and-done" dessert. Provide shots of espresso for each diner and let them dip their mascarpone-coated ladyfingers. Not only will this add an element of classic tiramisu, but it will also give the diner a sugary and creamy espresso shot to sip after dessert.

Cooking Notes:

- *When working with mascarpone, make sure all the ingredients are at room temperature to prevent the cheese from curdling. Mascarpone left out for 3 to 4 hours should do the trick. While similar to cream cheese, mascarpone is more fragile and can easily break if overstirred or whipped.*

- *There are two types of Marsala: dry and sweet. This recipe calls for dry Marsala. Sweet Marsala will make this dip too sugary.*

- *If you plan to serve this dip with sugary cookies—like vanilla wafers or chocolate chip cookies—consider decreasing the amount of sugar. Vanilla wafers can replace ladyfingers, but they are a bit more sugary.*

Yields 6–8 SERVINGS

16 oz (454 g) mascarpone, at room temperature

½ cup (100 g) sugar

2 tbsp (30 ml) espresso (or very strong coffee), at room temperature

2 tbsp (30 ml) dry Marsala, at room temperature

Cocoa powder

Ladyfingers, to serve

In a large bowl, combine the mascarpone, sugar, espresso and Marsala. Gently fold together until combined.

Sift a thin layer of cocoa powder onto the bottom of a serving bowl or individual serving bowls. Add the mascarpone dip to the bowl and top with a second sifted layer of cocoa powder.

Place into the refrigerator and chill until firm, at least 2 to 3 hours. Serve with the ladyfingers and optional espresso shots.

Fiori di Sicilia Panna Cotta

Panna cotta is a delight to make and even more of a joy to serve. This quick-cooking recipe combines whipping cream, gelatin, sugar and a playful flavoring to yield a most delicate and delicious pudding-like treat. It requires minimal ingredients and little active cook time. The decadence and unfamiliarity of cooked cream is a treat to many diners, making it a memorable dessert and one where you—the cook—appear kitchen accomplished.

Cooking Notes:

- *Fiori di Sicilia extract is a lovely, aromatic extract that has orange, floral and vanilla notes. It can be found at specialty food stores or online.*

- *If you are working with gelatin for the first time, don't fret. It's easy to use.*

- *Panna cotta is rich and heavy. Be sure to use small portion sizes so as to not overwhelm the diner.*

Yields 8–10 SERVINGS

4 cups (960 ml) heavy cream

1 tbsp (11 g) gelatin

¾ cup (160 g) sugar

½ tsp Fiori di Sicilia extract

Pour the cream into a large saucepan and sprinkle the gelatin evenly on top. Do not stir. Let the gelatin sit on top of the cream for 10 minutes.

Place the pan on the cooktop and turn the heat to medium. Stir the mixture. Once the cream is warm, about 5 minutes, add the sugar and the Fiori di Sicilia extract. Do not let the mixture boil.

Continually stir the cream until the gelatin dissolves completely, 5 to 8 minutes. The mixture will look clumpy at first, but as you continue to stir the cream, the mixture will become smooth and the gelatin will dissolve.

Pour the cooked cream into individual serving bowls, between ¼ to ½ cup (60 to 120 ml) per bowl. Alternatively, it can be placed into a large serving bowl. Cover the bowls and refrigerate at least 6 hours before serving.

Once the panna cotta is set, serve cold with toppings of your choice.

Peppermint Meringue Cookies

Meringues are one of the simplest desserts. Reminiscent of an after-dinner mint, these cookies are great to keep around the house, serve at dinner parties or give as gifts. They can keep for up to two weeks if stored in an airtight container. Since meringues use only egg whites, there will be leftover egg yolks that can be used in other recipes, like Cauliflower Gratin (page 86) or Wedding Cake Ice Cream (page 138). Waste not, want not.

Cooking Notes:

- *What makes meringues finicky is that if the egg whites are overwhipped, they cannot be recovered. Once stiff peaks form, stop whisking. The whisking time will vary with the mixer used and the kitchen environment. A hot and humid kitchen yields a different result than a cool and dry kitchen.*

- *When forming the cookies, there are options. While a pastry bag creates uniform, well-shaped cookies, it can be difficult to use if you are not a seasoned baker. Two soup spoons or an ice cream scoop can also yield consistently sized cookies with less fuss. The cookies will be more abstract in shape, but this is okay. Consistent size is the goal, not pretty shapes—which will come with practice.*

- *If the meringue cookies come out sticky, they are undercooked and need a longer oven rest time. The longer the oven time, the crispier the meringue.*

Yields 35–40 COOKIES

4 egg whites

¼ tsp cream of tartar

¾ cup (160 g) sugar

⅛ tsp peppermint extract

⅛ tsp vanilla extract

Adjust the racks in the oven so that one is at the top level and another is at the bottom level. Heat the oven to 225°F (107°C). Line two sheet pans with parchment paper or use silicone baking mats. Set aside.

Place the egg whites and cream of tartar into a large bowl. Using a stand or electric mixer, whisk the ingredients at medium-high speed for 2 to 2½ minutes, until peaks begin to form.

Turn off the mixer and quickly pour the sugar and peppermint and vanilla extracts into the mixture. Resume whisking at medium-high speed until stiff peaks form, about 30 seconds.

Using two soup spoons, scoop out one portion of meringue with one spoon. Push off the meringue with the other spoon, placing it onto the parchment-lined sheet pan. Continue until all the meringue is used. Place the sheet pans into the oven and bake for 1 hour.

After the hour, turn off the oven and let the meringues cool in the oven for 1½ to 2 hours. Remove from the oven and store in an airtight container for up to two weeks.

acknowledgments

This book was developed during a pandemic—when families stayed close together, gathering around tables, seeking comfort and familiarity through home-cooked meals. The spring and summer of 2020 captured the power of a shared table amidst the turmoil of the unknown. Food is comforting and healing. I had the benefit of writing a book at a time when home-cooked meals became a necessity overnight. The food in this book reflects that.

Recipe after recipe graced our family's table during the book's development to provide not only physical sustenance for the day, but also emotional support for the season. While our table was laden with recipes that now fill the chapters of this book, our hearts were nourished daily by home-cooked meals and meaningful time together. The writing of this book during an unprecedented season confirmed my conviction that sharing food with others brings hope and comfort. Our dinnertime lingered over food—it was full of conversation, laughter and thoughtful opinions. The strength and unity that followed this daily congregation will have a lasting impact. These mealtime moments that surrounded the food developed for this book make the recipes even more endearing.

This book could not have been created without the editors, designers, marketers and publishing team at Page Street Publishing Co., specifically Jenna Fagan. Thank you for seeing the potential and value of my work. This anthology exists because of your trust in me. Thank you for the support and opportunity.

During the development of this book, my husband and most constant partner was always present. Thank you, Randy, for being you. Your knowledge of food, cooking technique, grammar and undeniable humor have been key to the growth of this book. Your encouragement—whether pressing me forward or helping me to stop—was life-giving. I could not have built this book without you. The depth of my love for you has no limit.

Two other recipe tasters were by my side during the construction of this book. Katherine and Eli, thank you for your carefree, joyful expressions of thoughtful opinion. Your young palates have no boundaries and your excitement for this book will forever fill my heart with cherished memories. This book could not have been written without your daily energy and confirmation that this book contains tasty recipes. You both are so very loved.

Thank you, dad, for being a 1980s pioneer amateur food photographer—snapping photographs of dinner whether at home or out, your excitement for food left an imprint on me. From a young age, you and mom instilled in me a romantic pursuit of dreams—thank you to you both for always believing that I could and would achieve my goals. Mama, your unconditional and devoted love helped to shape me into the woman I am today; I miss you. To JoDee and Mindy—thank you for allowing me to flood your inboxes with messages showcasing each day's progress or rambling about deadlines and stress. The world has not known two better sisters, and your encouragement has been great. Aunt Linda, you have been my constant cheerleader, instilling words of encouragement and love, and I could not have asked for a better aunt. Aunt Janie, my memories are full of family gatherings surrounded by you, mom and Granny at the helm—reeling in the cousins and providing us with an abundant table. Your loyalty and love is constant, so thank you. To Dolores and Bobby, thank you for always letting me feed you and send you home with a plethora of food. Your continuous support and love is dear to our family.

To the friends who have been by my side since before my pursuit of food began. Abi, your most devoted and loving friendship has been a light. Our fun began over a pint of ice cream and has continued to include some of the most fantastic meals and moments—experiences that will continue all our days. Megan, adventures and thoughtful conversations with you have filled my heart and mind for a lifetime, and your friendship makes life better. Ashley, your laugh is contagious and so is your strength. Your presence in my life is treasured. Ladies, your support and excitement for this book always came at the right moment.

Ridiculous title aside, to the Dinner Divas: Amanda, Jamie, Karen, Kristin, Lindsay and Megan—thank you for over 10 years of the best moments shared monthly around a table. Also, thank you for letting me constantly ask what is (or is not) stocked in your pantry while creating this book. Becky, thank you for always dreaming with me. Can we take another walk soon? Richi, thank you for speaking truth into my life, believing in my talents and pushing me forward to pursue A Pleasant Little Kitchen and the idea of a book. Jane, you opened the first door—my heart is forever grateful.

Thank you, Erin Booke, food editor at *The Dallas Morning News*, for your endless support, friendship and copy edits over the past years. You enhance my words and have given me a voice through monthly opportunities to develop recipes, write and photograph for *The Dallas Morning News*. It has been a highlight of my career. I am grateful to you and the entire staff for letting me share my love of food with our most-wonderful city.

To my friends who received leftovers from these recipe tests—thank you for not only taking the food out of my fridge but for also providing helpful feedback.

To the community of A Pleasant Little Kitchen, the most heartfelt thank you. Your excitement and commitment, whether for a new recipe on the website, a photograph on social media or my latest piece in *The Dallas Morning News*, is overwhelming. I could not have been able to pursue this dream without your encouragement.

Finally, to you, dear reader: It has been the highest honor to write this book. Thank you for welcoming me into your kitchen. I cannot wait to cook by your side.

about the author

Rebecca White is the creator and author of the long-standing and acclaimed website A Pleasant Little Kitchen. She is a frequent special contributor to *The Dallas Morning News,* where her recipes, stories and photography are published. Rebecca's work has been featured by local and national food media. Rebecca is a freelance recipe developer, food photographer and food writer. She lives in Dallas with her husband, two children and a Westie named Marcus Aurelius. She enjoys books, history, tennis and feeding people.

index